On the Road with the Archangel

ALSO BY FREDERICK BUECHNER

On the Road
with the
Archangel

A NOVEL

FREDERICK BUECHNER

HarperSanFrancisco
A Division of HarperCollins*Publishers*

HarperCollins Web Site: http://www.harpercollins.com

HarperCollins®, ☕®, and HarperSanFrancisco™ are trademarks of HarperCollins Publishers Inc.

FIRST EDITION

Designed by Laura Lindgren

Library of Congress Cataloging-in-Publication Data
Buechner, Frederick, 1926–
     On the road with the archangel : a novel / Frederick Buechner.—1st ed.
     ISBN 0–06–061125-1 (cloth)
     I. Title.
PS3552.U3505   1997
813'.54—dc21   97-4099

98 99 00 01 RRD(H) 10 9 8 7 6 5 4

To the memory of James Merrill,
who spoke with archangels,
and a friendship of fifty-five years.

CONTENTS

AUTHOR'S NOTE

The apocryphal Book of Tobit is generally believed to have been written in either Hebrew or Aramaic by an unknown author sometime during the second century B.C. The place of its composition may have been Jerusalem, Antioch, or Alexandria. Who knows?

The historical period of the book is bounded on one end by the year 722 B.C., when the Assyrians captured the Northern Kingdom of Israel and carried the cream of its population off to their capital city of Nineveh, and on the other by the year 612 B.C., when Nineveh itself was captured and razed by a coalition of Medes and Babylonians. The anonymous author was as cavalier about getting all his facts straight, however, as the Archangel Raphael in my version. He is hazy about which Assyrian king did what, he wrongly places the Tigris between Nineveh and Ecbatana, and from Ecbatana to Rages is not "a two days journey." He was more interested in telling a good story, and so, through the Archangel's lips, was I.

I have stuck as closely as possible to the narrative as he wrote it. I have not added any new characters except for such walk-ons as the blind beggar and the girl with the blue scarf. Even Edna's unpleasant maidservants are present in the original, as are also, of course, the dog, the sparrows, and the monstrous fish. I have also not omitted any characters, not even the treacherous Nadab despite the fact that his role is strictly peripheral. My description of the demon Asmodeus is based on the one given in the Book of Revelation, where he appears under the name of Abaddon or, in Greek, Apollyon. All other descriptions, both of physical appearance and of character, are my own though based on such clues as the original contains. Tobit's view of the Holy One as essentially the Scorekeeper is consistent with how he speaks of him in the original, and the brief extracts from his interminable prayer that I give in chapter 13 are verbatim from the Revised Standard Version of the Bible.

Such humor as my tale contains is also in keeping with the unknown author's spirit. I can't imagine his having described with a straight face how poor Raguel got up in the middle of the night to dig a grave for his son-in-law and then sent somebody else to fill it in an hour or so later when it turned out not to be needed. But in terms of what he had to say about the ways both of God and of humankind, he was entirely serious. And so am I.

O N E

Tobit Insulted

I AM RAPHAEL, ONE OF THE SEVEN ARCHANGELS WHO PASS IN and out of the presence of the Holy One, blessed be he. I bring him the prayers of all who pray and of those who don't even know that they're praying.

Some prayers I hold out as far from me as my arm will reach, the way a woman holds a dead mouse by the tail when she removes it from the kitchen. Some, like flowers, are almost too beautiful to touch, and others so aflame that I'd be afraid of their setting me on fire if I weren't already more like fire than I am like anything else. There are prayers of such power that you might almost say they carry me rather than the other way round—the way a bird with outstretched wings is carried higher and higher on the back of the wind. There are prayers so apologetic and shamefaced and halfhearted that they all but melt away in my grasp like sad little flakes of snow. Some prayers are very boring.

Would it surprise you to know that when I'm not carrying prayers, I often shake with laughter? It is the world that I laugh at and never more heartily than when I bring to mind the story that in good time I will tell you.

It is the story of a journey and a fish and a boy. It is the story of a demon with hair like a woman's and a lion's teeth, and of a chatterbox of a wife and a slender, dark-haired girl who loved her father. It is the story of a twitter of sparrows who never for a moment doubted that their chalky droppings were a gift for the world to treasure, and of a dog with the eyes of a saint and a lavender tongue, and of two bags of silver with their seals unbroken. And it is the story of how I got myself up as a young globe-trotter with a stout pair of boots and a sack full of road maps. You will say that they didn't have such things as stout boots and road maps in ancient Assyria, and the chances are you are right, but when you have seen as many Assyrias come and go as I have, you tend to lose track of details.

I say I will tell the story "in good time," by which I mean two things. First, I mean that eventually I will tell it. I mean that through all its twists and turns I will bring it to an end at last. Second, I mean that time itself is *good*, even the times when the dung heaps of Nineveh were littered with the variously strangled, eviscerated, dismembered cadavers of those imprudent enough to catch the bloodshot eye of Shalmaneser, or Sennacherib, or Esarhaddon, or whatever sociopath happened to be sitting on the throne at the moment with his face all but lost in the oily black ringlets of a lamb's-wool beard and on either hand a winged bull higher than a house who looked just like him.

The things that the world fills time with are enough to turn the heart to stone, but the goodness of time itself is as untouched by them as the freshness of a spring morning is untouched by the yelps from the scaffold. Time is good because the Holy One made it that way and then set the heavenly bodies wheeling through the sky so there would always be a way of marking its passage. Unfortunately, not even the most devout understand this for more than possibly a day or two out of the entire year when everything seems to be going their way. The rest of the year they go around like everybody else rolling their eyes and expecting terrible things to happen. When terrible things do happen, they fail to understand that for the most part they have brought them down on their own heads. They prefer to think that it is time itself that is terrible and that the terrible things are only another method by which the Holy One afflicts them for their sins.

Take Tobit for instance. He was blind as a bat when Anna, his wife, insulted him, but he rolled his eyes anyway because she had told him he was a fool, and he suspected that she might be right and that the Holy One agreed with her. She stood in the kitchen with her lower lip thrust forward in the way that she had and dressed him down so thoroughly that you would never have guessed that in her heart she was quite fond of him. She herself did not guess it, so carried away she was by the force of her own eloquence. Every month or so she was in the habit of doing something new and implausible with her hair because it was a way of using up some of her unspent energy. On this occasion she had dyed it as black as the king's beard and, except for a few corkscrew curls around her ears, had piled it high on her head with the use of some bone pins and a pair of ivory combs that one of the rich women she worked for had given her in a moment of uncharacteristic generosity. Not noticing the dog as she stormed out of the kitchen, she tripped over him. He was a large, mild-mannered dog with a coat as shaggy and gray as smoke who belonged to her son, Tobias. When he leapt to his feet to get out of her way, he knocked over a table piled with dirty dishes, and Tobit, who of course could see nothing of what had happened, concluded not unreasonably that she was in the process of adding to her insult by pulling the house down about their ears. It was the last straw, and once she had left, he groped his way through the wreckage to the outhouse behind the vine-covered wall in the courtyard, which a few years earlier had been the scene of his blinding. It was there that he uttered a prayer.

What he asked was to die as soon as possible rather than to endure any further indignities, and I carried his prayer into the Presence, together with another prayer almost exactly like it that at exactly the same moment was uttered in tears by a young woman who lived some miles away from Nineveh in the city of Ecbatana. It is with those two prayers for death that the story begins, but first it is necessary to move backward in time, whose goodness the young woman was as blind to as Tobit, who was of course blind to everything else as well, including the fact that even as his wife was insulting him, he was really as fond of her as she was of him though neither of them would ever have thought to mention it, least of all to each other or even to themselves. She had stuck with him through all the years of his blindness, even though it had come about through his own imprudence, and supported them both by doing mending and washing and occasional weaving for some of the ladies of the court who lived in the enormous warren of a palace that stretched some two miles along the banks of the river Tigris in a succession of columned halls whose walls were carved with the likeness of the king and his barbarous armies.

It was Sargon who had dreamed the palace up and worked great numbers of slaves half to death building it and Sargon too who had captured the Northern Kingdom of the Jews and carried off as many of them, including Tobit, as he believed might cause trouble if he left them behind. The Jews who could afford it were allowed to make the long northward journey on camelback or muleback or in wagons hired for the occasion, in which they rattled around like dice in a cup with as many of their possessions as they were able to salvage heaped around them and trying to keep their spirits up by singing patriotic songs, which only made matters worse by reminding them of the homeland they would in all likelihood never see again. The rest of them slogged along as best they could through the hills in a series of forced marches with Sargon's whip-wielding soldiers continually on the lookout for stragglers.

Although Tobit was a relatively young man at the time, he was already paunchy and balding with a small, round mouth and arched eyebrows that gave him a look of perpetual surprise. In moments of distraction, he had the habit of conducting an imaginary group of musicians such as he had often seen perform in the outer court of Solomon's temple in the years before his people were carried off. If things weren't going fast enough to suit him, he would chop impatiently at the air with his right hand or, if too fast, would pat it with both hands at once as delicately as a woman calming an overexcited child. With a finger at his lips, he would try to restrain the rams' horns or work the stringed psalteries to a crescendo by frantically sweeping them forward as if from a burning house. If things turned sour, you would have thought he was having a tooth drawn the way he would twist his face into a knot and wave his arms around. When he closed his eyes and showed his teeth in a rapturous smile at the restoration of harmony, he could have been lost in the act of love.

It was this eccentricity that first brought him to the attention of Sargon himself. Tobit and several other exiled Jews were at work repairing one of the outer walls of the palace where a chariot had turned the corner too sharply and broken off part of the lower hind leg of a stone bull. Tobit was standing somewhat apart, leading the invisible musicians with such abandon during a lull in the operation that the king, who happened to be passing by at the time, decided he must be a lunatic and had him brought before him later that day because lunatics were considered valuable either as a source of entertainment or as spokesmen of the gods.

Although frightened half out of his wits at finding himself in the presence of someone who at a whim could order him sawed in half, Tobit conducted himself with such becoming deference and good sense during the interview that the king decided that, although he was regrettably as sane as anybody else, he might still be useful to him. He spoke the Assyrian tongue with considerable fluency. He stood his ground. He had the plump, unguarded face of a man not clever enough to be anything but honest. And thus Sargon, who was in a rare mood of benevolence brought on by the not entirely natural death that very morning of one of his wives, ordered him taken off the repair crew and dispatched instead to neighboring Media to buy a quantity of pistachio nuts and honey for the royal table. Tobit struck such a good bargain and gave such a thorough accounting of the transaction on his return that Sargon appointed him one of his chief purchasing agents, and it was not long before he and Anna and their son, Tobias, became as prosperous as any of the Jews in Nineveh. At the same time, he did not forget his less fortunate compatriots, and in between buying expeditions he became a familiar sight as he made his way through the rat-infested hovels down by the river where most of them lived, bringing them baskets of food from his own table and distributing clothes that either he and his family had discarded or that he was able to cadge from merchants eager to stand well with someone who was able to throw the king's business their way.

All of this he did in broad daylight in full view of his captors, who considered it only another of his crotchets and just as harmless as the way he occasionally flung his arms around through the air like a madman. But burying the bodies of the dead was another matter entirely, and this he did only in the darkness of night with a sack over his head in which he had Anna cut him three holes, two for his eyes and one to breathe through. This not only kept him from being recognized but also tended to send flying away in terror anybody he happened to meet who took him for some kind of ghoul instead of the good-hearted soul he was. Jews were always being executed under one pretext or another, and part of the punishment was to have their strangled bodies not given a decent burial but thrown in a heap like garbage outside the city walls or simply left in the streets somewhere or another where passers-by tried to ignore them. So off Tobit would go with the sack over his head and a shovel over his shoulder even though he well knew that if anyone caught him at it, he would soon end up on the garbage heap with the others. Anna told him that only a fool risks his life for the dead and tried to stop him. Tobias tried to stop him too although he was usually so slow to respond to things that there were some who thought he was softheaded. At the sight of the shovel, even the smoke-colored dog tried to stop him. Courteous and retiring as he was, he would rear himself up on his hind legs with his head on a level with Tobit's and plant his shaggy paws on his chest in an effort to keep him from going out the door.

When Sargon was killed in battle and his pickled head kicked around like an inflated bladder by the winning side, he was succeeded by his son Sennacherib, who with the lamb's-wool beard tied in place and wearing the same beehive-shaped crown low on his brow looked so like his father that most of the simple-minded folk he ruled hardly noticed the difference. He was kept so busy waging war with his Babylon-ian neighbors that for several years he had no time to give to the rumors that some troublemaker was breaking the law by burying the bodies of executed Jews, but the day finally came when one of his spies identified the troublemaker as Tobit, and the king paused long enough in his military duties to order him arrested immediately and all his property confis-cated. Luckily for Tobit, one of the court ladies had lost her heart to his son, Tobias. Tobias, whom I was soon to take under my wing with the most unexpected consequences, was a slow-talking, sleepy-eyed young man with a shy smile, and fearing that he might end up on the scaffold with his father, she sent word that disaster was about to befall them. Anna told her husband that it was exactly what she had always said was going to happen, and the three of them beat the arrival of the arresting officer by little more than an hour, making their escape to the mountains of Ararat, where the dog took delight in racing through the snow at astonishing speeds with his long tail arched over his back like a pennant.

The second stroke of luck was that Sennacherib was murdered by one of his sons, and the third was that Esarhaddon, his successor, appointed as his cupbearer, keeper of the signet, and second only to himself in power, a Jew named Ahikar, who was Tobit's nephew. Many made fun of Ahikar behind his back, and it was hard for me not to sympathize with them. In a voice as deep as a kettledrum, he spoke Assyrian with an impossible accent, had the matted hair and complacent smirk of a sheep, and walked with his toes turned outward, but Esarhaddon recognized that not only was he shrewder than any of his other counselors but as a Jew had the added advantage of belonging to none of the vying factions. Ahikar, in turn, recognized that Esarhaddon was as given to unabashed fraudulence and psychotic rages and hallucinations of grandeur as his predecessors, but he somehow managed never to let it ruffle him or to distract him from his resolve to be the one voice of sanity and moderation that ever reached the king's ear. Choosing the moment when Esarhaddon had just received some unusually encouraging omens from Sin, the moon god of Haran, he interceded for his uncle Tobit, pointing out how effectively he had served both

Esarhaddon's father and grandfather before him, and the command was promptly given that Tobit was to be allowed to return to Nineveh on guarantee of good behavior from that day forward. It was then that luck turned against him.

Restored to much of his former prosperity, he invited a number of friends to his house for the feast of Pentecost. The table was laid with a crimson cloth. The kitchen was ablaze with scented oil lamps. A lamb was roasted and served up with bitter herbs. Anna baked the bread without leaven, and Tobit himself saw to it that the wine cups were never empty. All in all there was such an abundance of good things to eat and to drink that there was vastly more than enough to go round, and turning to Tobias, who was more or less resisting the efforts of two young women to string a garland of flowers around his neck, he told him to go down to the hovels by the river and bring back any poor Jews he happened to meet there.

It was not long before Tobias returned on the run, his eyes wide as a fawn's. He said that he had found the blue-faced body of one of their people thrown into the street with the livid scar of the executioner's rope circling his neck like the garland. Without taking so much as another mouthful, Tobit sprang from his seat, ran out into the city, and when he found what he was after hid it in a dense thicket of willows by the river's edge. As soon as darkness fell and without even bothering to put the sack over his head, he went back with his shovel and buried it.

When he appeared at the feast again all covered with

mud and his sweaty face glistening, everybody knew immediately what he had been up to. Some of them shrugged their shoulders and laughed. Others, including Tobias, praised him for his daring. The dog flattened himself on the hearth and put his paws over his eyes. Anna threw her hands into the air. Because he had been defiled by touching the dead, Tobit himself washed thoroughly from head to toe and then left the house to sleep out what remained of the night in the courtyard so he would not defile anyone else. He lay down by the vine-covered wall for shelter in case it rained, and because it was warm and there was little air stirring, he neglected to cover his face.

Now enter the sparrows.

Perhaps the Holy One created them in such great numbers to make up to them for their being in every other way so unremarkable. They were small and drab with brown feathers and dingy white breasts and spent their lives either darting through the air to no particular purpose or squabbling. Sometimes they bathed themselves in the dust by hunkering down and fanning it over their heads with their wings. They had no memorable song like other birds, but as long as it was daylight, they were never still. They twittered or chirruped or went *teck teck* over and over again in a hoarse, recriminatory way as they fixed each other with their indignant little eyes. Only at night did they fall silent, and that is why Tobit gave no thought to them as he stretched himself out under the vines where a flock of them had made their nests.

Even if he had given thought to them, it would have made no difference because he had no idea what went on in their heads. Maybe because the rest of the world pays so little attention to them, sparrows have an unusually high self-regard, and since, with night having fallen, they were not of a mind to beguile him with what they thought of as the sweet sound of their voices raised in song, the next greatest favor they could think to do him was to scatter their white droppings on him while he slept with all the care of priests scattering incense on the flames of an altar. Some of their droppings fell on his uncovered face, and when he awoke shortly after dawn, he could not tell whether it was night or day because of the white films on his eyes.

Anna led him by the hand to a physician who treated him with all manner of herbs such as garlic and rue and mandrake, but nothing he could find to do made the slightest difference, and the films remained. His influential nephew Ahikar arranged for him to be seen by the chief of the king's Persian magicians, but no spell the old man cast, no evil-smelling vapors he blew into his face through the thigh bone of an ass, no spirit he was able to summon up from the shadows proved any more efficacious than the herbs, and it was finally concluded by everyone that Tobit was permanently blind.

Since he was no longer able to make purchasing expeditions for Esarhaddon, it was at this point that Anna started mending and laundering the court ladies' clothes, which

Tobias, the dog at his heels, would bring back to her in the two large baskets that hung from the yoke on his shoulders. She also became adept at weaving the fringed wool shawls that were in vogue at the time, and what with one thing or another, she earned enough to maintain the family in a fairly respectable state.

For Tobit, the worst part of being blind was not the inconvenience of it but the humiliation. It never seems to have occurred to him that the white films on his eyes had come about as the result of his own carelessness. Instead, like the rest of the pious, he believed that it is the Holy One who brings all such disasters down on the heads of his people as a method of punishing them either for their own misdeeds if they have committed any recently or for the misdeeds of their ancestors. They believed that the One who created time in its goodness and set the world afloat on it like a flowered barge is as ill-tempered and irrational and vengeful as one of their own kings. Yet they never ceased singing his praises even so, adjuring each other to love him with all their might when they had every reason in the world to hide from him in terror. It is no wonder that even in the Presence itself, I find myself shaking with laughter. Unseemly as it may appear, it is surely less so than being perpetually dissolved in tears.

Tobit knew that all his friends and neighbors would be sure that either he or his forbears had done something scabrous to merit the blindness that had come upon him, so he stayed mostly in his house to avoid their derisive glances and rarely went out even into his own courtyard, which held bad memories for him anyway.

Then one day Anna brought home a goat. Tobit could not see its long, drooping ears and bony rump, but from the rattle of its hooves on the kitchen floor and its nervous bleating, he knew immediately what it was. Convinced in his bitterness that no good thing could possibly befall him because of his sins, he accused Anna of having stolen it. On the contrary, she answered him with her face flushed, one of the court ladies had presented it to her as a gift in addition to her wages. If he did not appreciate all the work she was doing, there were others who did.

This only increased Tobit's depression by reminding him that he was no longer capable of doing any work at all except for occasionally washing the dishes, most of which he broke, and from the way he screwed up his face and slashed at the air with his hands it was clear that the invisible musicians had gone berserk. She had stolen it without question, he repeated, and she must return it at once to its rightful owners before the law was upon them. It was then that Anna changed the course of all of their lives, including eventually even my own, by insulting him.

"You think you know everything," she said in her lowest voice, which was also her most dangerous, and rapped his head with a wooden spoon to ensure his closest attention. "But the fact of the matter is that you know as little as your eyes can see. Your years of good deeds and the endless graves you have dug have counted for nothing. You have made a laughing stock of us all."

As soon as she was gone, leading the goat on its tether behind her, he groped his way into the outhouse where he prayed to die rather than to submit himself any longer to her outrageous accusations.

"Command that I now be released from my dishonor," he said. "Do not turn your face away from me."

Like the rest of the devout, he was incapable of understanding that the Holy One's face is never turned away but constantly looks down on all creatures with a beneficence that they are too busy apologizing for their unworthiness and performing their good works and assuring Heaven of their unfailing devotion to notice.

It was with this dismal prayer, and another just like it uttered by a young woman named Sarah at precisely the same moment, that the story finally begins.

But, first, the young woman named Sarah.

TWO

Sarah Accused

L IKE TOBIAS, SARAH WAS AN ONLY CHILD. HER FATHER WAS
Raguel, a quiet, retiring man who stood scarcely taller than a
child himself and made me always feel like the Tower of Babel
in his presence. Her mother was Edna, who was rarely quiet
except when there was no one she felt like talking to. Everyone, including Sarah, was devoted to Raguel and pitied him
because of his wife. It was not just that she talked so much but
that she did so in a peculiarly suffocating way. She explained
things that a dunce could have understood without half trying. She advised people to follow certain courses of action that
were precisely the ones they had been following all their lives.
She expounded platitudes at exhausting length as if she had

discovered them. She sounded for all the world like a child dressed up in her mother's clothes playing at being grown up, and when people saw her coming down the street, they ducked into doorways or pulled their head cloths over their faces in hopes she would not recognize them. The truth is that it was less the world than it was her own childish self that she was trying to convince that she was as mature and sensible as everybody else, and none knew better than she did how completely she failed in both instances.

"Have you any idea how it feels to walk into a room full of people and know that none of them can stand you?" she said one day to Raguel, her husband. Instead of answering the question, he told her she mustn't think thoughts like that, but if he had answered it honestly, he would have had to say that when you came right down to it, he had no idea what it felt like because when he entered the room, virtually everybody was pleased and no one more so than his daughter, Sarah.

There are trees that look like her somewhat, slender, dark-leaved trees such as grow by the banks of rivers and are dappled by the light that glances off the water. Men and women alike were refreshed by her still, green presence, and even old people felt young again in her shade. Edna was eager to marry her off, and she had two main reasons for being so. The first was that in her own tangled way she loved her daughter and hoped to go to her grave knowing that she had a decent man at her side to take care of her. If he was rich and handsome enough to arouse the neighbors' envy, so much the better. The other reason was that as soon as she possibly could, she wanted to get her out of the house where she was as much admired as Edna was shunned like the pox and where she was as obviously her father's favorite as her father was obviously hers. Edna wanted a husband for her daughter more than she wanted anything else, and no less than seven times she succeeded in finding her one only to have the triumph turn almost immediately to wormwood and gall.

What with all the various practical matters to be taken into consideration, most particularly financial matters, not to mention the law that as a Jew Sarah could marry only within her father's tribe, it was no easy task to find men who were eligible, but with the persistence of an invading army, Edna managed over the space of a few years to root the seven of them out one after another.

They came in varying degrees of presentability. The kindest one had a squint, and the most entertaining was the same age as Raguel. By far the handsomest of the lot was a compulsive womanizer, and the richest a widower with a houseful of quarrelsome children. And so on. In each case the marriage contract was drawn up and signed by both fathers, and to the squealing of horns and thudding of goatskin drums, the bridal pair was paraded to the chamber that had been prepared with sweet-smelling herbs and charms that assured fertility. And each time tragedy followed.

The way it came about was this. Sarah did not want to be married because she could not bear to leave her father to the mercy of a woman she feared would drive him out of his wits as soon as there was no one else left in the house to harangue except for him. She also did not want to be married because the thought of losing her maidenhood in the embrace of a virtual stranger not only filled her with revulsion and fright in itself but also struck her as a betrayal of the love she had for the small, gentle man who in so many ways depended as much on her as she did on him.

So with the aid of an overweight Egyptian woman the color of a charred loaf who eked out her meager living as a midwife by dabbling in the more sinister forms of magic, she summoned to her rescue none other than the lord of the demons himself, who is sometimes called Asmodeus, which means the Destroyer, and sometimes by one of his other names, which are as numerous as the flies that swarm on a dead bull's carcass. I do not know why the Holy One permits such creatures to exist because I have never spoken of them in the Presence for fear that his forgiveness of my bad taste would consume me like fire. Perhaps the light of his glory casts shadows whose very darkness bears witness to its brilliance although the demons themselves put it the other way round, of course, and claim that it is the darkness that is from everlasting to everlasting and the light of glory only the flash of a tear in the eyes of the eternally doomed. But such mysteries as these are not to be solved by clever words. Even the angels can only stand dumb before them.

Asmodeus was able to assume as many different forms

as the names he was known by, and he was constantly assuming one or the other of them because otherwise he was so intimidating to behold that everyone he approached fled in terror. This gratified his vanity, to be sure, but it also left him feeling depressed and lonely. If he had appeared before Sarah as his true self, what she would have seen was a creature with its head and shoulders covered by a carapace that glinted like gold, the narrow, transparent wings of a dragonfly that clattered like chariots in battle when it flew, and a muscular flap of a tail not unlike a lobster's that it could curl and uncurl in the blink of an eye with a scorpion's sting at the end. She would have seen a face that was more or less human but with a lion's fangs in its mouth and the flowing tresses of a woman.

What he contrived to have her see instead was a very tall, very bony young man whose unusually long hair was gathered in a knot at his nape and whose bold smile revealed a set of strong teeth remarkable for their brightness. Even so, the sight of him was more than enough to send the Egyptian woman streaking out of her cluttered booth as fast as her bulk would allow, but so acute was Sarah's need for help on the eve of the first of her seven weddings that she stood her ground and laid her plight before him.

She explained that she had nothing personal against her prospective husband—the kind one with a squint was the first of the seven—but that the thought of abandoning her father for him was unbearable. She explained that though her mother had many good points, for Raguel to live with her all by himself in their modest quarters would almost surely destroy him. With her eyes lowered and her voice almost too quiet to hear, she added how she felt about giving herself to a man the very next day in a chamber filled with sweet-smelling herbs and gris-gris of various sorts guaranteed to produce fertility. She then covered her face with her hands, and the tears seeped out between her fingers like drops of rain through the leaves of a tree.

Asmodeus was moved in a way to suggest that not even the lords of darkness are entirely bereft of some glimmer of the radiance they abhor. With one hand as light as a dragon-fly's wing on her shoulder, he assured her that he would see to the matter and she had no need to fear the man who was soon to stand naked before her. When she uncovered her face to plead that he deal with him mercifully, he said that whatever he did would be done with irreproachable tact.

On the morning after the wedding when Sarah's cries brought both Edna and Raguel running in a panic to find her standing pale beside the bridegroom's rigid body, there was no mark of foul play upon him except for a single pink dot like a sting on the back of his neck which nobody noticed. It was assumed by everybody that the blissful prospect before him had proved too much and his heart had simply stopped beating.

At the second and even the third wedding, at each of which the nearly identical scene took place, the Jews of

Ecbatana continued to advance this theory with only a few of the more outspoken among them whispering to one another that the bride's demure appearance must conceal a voracity that was more than even a healthy young man could attempt to satisfy without fatal consequences. But when the fourth wedding came along and yet another body was carried out of the ill-starred chamber, it was concluded by everyone including Edna and Raguel that something unearthly was surely involved.

Then it was that Sarah told at least part of the truth. She said that it was the demon Asmodeus who was to blame and that it was only her fear of some hair-raising reprisal that had kept her from saying so earlier. No one, of course, was more horrified than her parents although their horror stemmed from different sources—Raguel's from his passionate concern for his daughter's safety and Edna's from her ever darkening suspicion that at this rate there would never be a husband to take her off their hands once and for all.

Needless to say the difficulty of finding further candidates was increased so greatly by what had happened to the others that even Edna's powers were taxed to their limit, but somehow or other she managed to sign up the fifth, sixth, and seventh by promising that all conceivable precautions would be taken to protect them. Armed with every sort of weapon they could lay their hands on, she and Raguel, as well as three or four close relatives, stood guard all night as near the bridal chamber as their natural modesty permitted. They also enlisted the aid of several foreigners who were known for their skill in casting out demons including, ironically, the Egyptian woman, who of course made no mention of her earlier dealings with Sarah. But Asmodeus was able to pass through all their defenses like a shadow, and the last three bridegrooms went the way of the earlier four.

It was Edna's two maidservants who came up with a new theory that almost proved the undoing of Sarah. The tall one with the shoulders of a wrestler and a voice almost as deep as Ahikar's looked more like a man than a woman, and the short one who took small, tripping steps when she walked looked less like a woman than a bird. They had not only noticed the pink dot on the back of the men's necks but, in the case of the last two or three, thought they could detect also a certain discoloration around the throat which led them to conclude that they had been strangled. Furthermore, they decided, there was no need to dream up some bugaboo as the strangler when it was much more plausibly a human. Their final verdict was that it was Sarah herself.

They admitted to each other that they couldn't imagine where so slender a young woman had found the strength, and her motive struck them as equally puzzling, but they had long held a grudge against her for all the extra work that her continuing presence in the house caused them and would probably go on causing them for years to come the way things were going, and gradually, all evidence to the contrary notwithstanding, they talked each other into believing that her guilt was as plain as the nose on her face.

For weeks they kept this strictly to themselves, but one day when Edna had given them both a good slapping because they had taken so long cleaning Sarah's room that dinner was delayed by an hour, they could remain silent no longer. They waited till the young woman summoned them to comb her hair and help her to bed and then at last confronted her.

"It's you what done it, and don't try to tell us different," the tall one boomed out like a fist pounding on a barrel.

"Seven of them dead as mackerels, and you'll soon be too if there's justice in Heaven," the short one chirped like a sparrow.

"May we never see a son of yours," said the tall one, and the short one echoed her with "Nor a daughter neither."

Then they both of them burst into tears at the terrible words they had spoken, and Sarah fled from the room with her feet bare and her nightdress fluttering apart over her freckled young breasts.

She knew the two dreadful women had lied. It was Asmodeus who had done it. But she also knew they had told the truth because it was she who, without actually spelling it out, had asked him to. She then went straight out into the sheep shed where no one would be likely to look for her and prepared to hang herself. She had gone so far as trying unsuccessfully to throw a length of rope over one of the beams when she suddenly saw that it would break her father's heart and he would live in disgrace for the rest of his days. So leaving the rope in a tangle on the straw, she knelt down beside it and prayed.

Like Tobit miles away in Nineveh, she asked the Holy One to take her life because of the terrible stain on her honor. If for some reason this was not possible, she asked him at least to see to it that people should look on her with pity and that no reproach should ever fall upon Raguel. She prayed for her seven dead husbands also.

The bravest thing she did was to pray even for Asmodeus because for all she could tell, the mere mention of his name might be enough to bring the Holy One's wrath down upon her. She knew, she said, that he had done what he had done solely as a favor to her. What she did not know was that after no more than their seven brief meetings, he had fallen in love with her because she had called upon him. Nor did she know that in a secret place in her heart that she rarely dared enter, she was close to falling in love with him because he had answered her call.

I took her prayer in my left hand and Tobit's in my right and carried them both to the Most High where I set them down at his feet as softly as the snow falls.

"Now go back," was the command I heard like the rushing of wind through a forest. "Set everything right."

At that precise moment, Tobit reentered the kitchen from the outhouse where he had been praying, and Sarah the daughter of Raguel came back from the sheep shed.

THREE

The Commission
of Tobias

Tobit felt sure that his prayer would be answered and that there could be no more than a few weeks left for him to live. The time had come for him to think of his family's welfare after he was gone, and as he turned his mind in that direction, he closed his blind eyes and listened, with one finger raised, to the lullabying of the invisible harps and the flutes' melancholy warble. Waiting till Anna had gone off to the market in search of fresh dyes for the fringed shawls she was weaving, he called out the window to Tobias, who was sitting in the courtyard with one of the young women who had tried to force the garland upon him at Pentecost.

The boy was quick to answer his father's summons. He knew that Tobit was in low spirits, and pity welled up in his eyes as he stood there waiting for him to speak. Forgetting that Tobit could not see him, he held his hands out to either side, palms upward, to indicate that he was ready to do whatever was asked of him. Tobit asked him to sit down and pay the closest attention.

The first thing Tobit told him was that he must be sure above all things to take good care of his mother, Anna, although he had every reason to believe that she was entirely capable of taking excellent care of herself. She had never looked more so than during those days immediately following her refusal to return the goat that Tobit had accused her of stealing. She ran her increasingly successful business with her lower lip thrust even farther forward than usual and had colored her hair a strident henna, stiffening it with sheep-dip and pinning it into an enormous loop that hung down her back like a hangman's noose.

"Honor her all the days of her life," Tobit said, "because she suffered great pain bearing you."

This was what Anna had always claimed anyway, but as a blast from the rams' horns reminded Tobit that actually the birth had been a relatively easy one, he raised one hand to silence them.

"When she dies," he said, "you must make sure to bury her at my side." He went on then to explain to the boy where, when the time came, he would find the shovel that ever since the white films appeared on his eyes there had been no occasion to use.

"Whatever you say," Tobias answered with a gay smile on his lips at the thought of his mother's ever consenting to be buried anywhere. He was sitting on a stool near the stove, and the dog was on his haunches beside him with his bearded chin on his master's knee.

Satisfied that all would be well with his widow, Tobit turned then to more general admonitions.

"Never forget for one instant that the eye of the Holy One is upon you," he said, and for a moment the look of surprise that was usually conveyed by his round mouth and arched eyebrows became instead the look of someone who has just stepped on a rusty nail.

"Never think you can get away with anything, and remember the score is always being kept. I think particularly about women," he said, "because women are always hanging around you for some reason or other. You must never take advantage of them. More to the point, you must never let them take advantage of you."

Tobias's smile grew gayer still as he thought about women. He wondered if the one he had just left outside was planning to take advantage of him.

"I do not need to warn you about drink," Tobit said, "because as far as I know, that has never been one of your problems. But you are bound to change as you grow older just like everybody else, and if ever you find yourself growing too fond of it, limit yourself to no more than one cup for every guest at your table. If you eat by yourself, that means none at all. It is a rule that has stood me in good stead my whole life."

He paused then for a moment or two and listened to the bickering of the sparrows. He had had Tobias take all their nests down from the vine-covered wall and scatter lime on top of it to discourage their return, but there seemed to be more of them than ever, and the courtyard was scattered everywhere with their chalky droppings.

"I am not saying that you are soft-headed or anything like that," Tobit said, "but you have always been somewhat slower to understand things than most people, so never be bashful about seeking advice from the older and wiser. My nephew Ahikar comes to mind, for instance. No one in Nineveh knows his way around the way Ahikar does, and no one is in a better position to put in a good word for you with the king, although when it comes to the king, by far the best thing you can do is steer as clear of him as you possibly can."

The dog had stretched himself out on the hearth by now and was grooming his feathery belly with long sweeps of his tongue.

"Your mother never tires of telling me that my good deeds were what brought about my ruin," he said. "Practically speaking, I suppose she is right. She was certainly right when it came to digging holes for their bodies. But I wouldn't have done any different even so, and I want you to follow in my footsteps. Never forget the ones who are worse off than you are because the Holy One, blessed be he, will put it all down to your credit and because someday, who knows, you may find yourself one of them."

It was at this point that something moving in the courtyard caught Tobias's eye, and he tiptoed as far as the open doorway to see what it might be. He had thought the young woman had long since left, but she was still there sitting under a mulberry tree and waving a blue scarf lazily back and forth in hopes that it might catch his eye. When she saw him appear in the doorway, she did something with her tongue and her lips that made him blush like a young woman himself and return straightaway to his seat before his father, who had been talking the whole time, knew he was gone.

He had been talking about money.

"Ten talents of silver," he said. "It is nothing to sneeze at, a sum like that. Your mother couldn't earn even a tenth as much if she worked all day long every day for the rest of her life. So don't come back without it. I will give you what you need as I have told you, and we'll find someone to help."

"I beg your pardon?" Tobias said.

Emboldened by his brief appearance a few moments before, the young woman had come to within only a few feet of the door. With an end of the blue scarf in each hand, she had stretched it tight across the small of her back and was pulling it now this way, now that way, as if she was drying herself after a bath.

Tobias tried the best he could to focus his mind while his father, with pointed slowness, repeated what he had been saying when the boy was otherwise occupied.

"It was years ago, on the king's business in Media, that I left the two sacks with my friend Gabael for safekeeping because you never knew what kind of hornet's nest you might run into those days when the wars were going on everywhere," he said. "Gabael was always honest in his dealings with me, but I sealed the sacks anyway just to play it safe and made him give me a receipt, which even you will have no difficulty getting for me now if you can only keep your mind from wandering. Under our bed there is the chest where your mother keeps her wigs, and if you dig down to the bottom, you should be able to find it."

Steering as wide a berth as he could around the doorway and keeping his eyes straight forward, Tobias did as he was told and was back within moments with the clay tablet in his hand which he dropped in his father's lap.

"What will you do with it now?" the boy asked, and Tobit clapped both hands to his ears as though at that moment someone had crashed the cymbals together just as someone else had struck the drum with such force that it burst to pieces.

"Have you heard a single word I've said?" he asked.

Tobias ran his hand through his mop of hair and cast a furtive glance over his shoulder in the direction of the blue scarf.

"What I'll do with it now is give it to you," Tobit said as though he was speaking to the deaf, and at the same time he held it out in the general vicinity of his son, who took it from him.

"What *you* will do with it," he said, "is find your way somehow to the city of Rages in Media. Once you are there, please God, you will ask how to get to the house of Gabael the son of Gabrias, who was one of our people. You will then ask him to give you the silver and bring it back here as fast as your large feet will carry you. It will be more than enough to last you and your mother the rest of your lives."

"How will I know what roads to take to Media, which as far as I know is on the other side of the world?" Tobias asked. "It is confusing enough just to find my way through the streets of Nineveh to pick up the laundry for Mother."

"You have always been lucky," his father said. "Someone is bound to turn up to show you the way. The dog has a better head on his shoulders than many I can think of. Maybe he will help too."

The dog, whom Tobias had never bothered to give a name, raised his head at the word "dog" and grinned up at his master with his lavender tongue dangling.

"How can I be sure your friend will give me the money when he has never set eyes on me in his life?"

"Tell me what you have in your hand," Tobit said.

In one hand Tobias had a lock of his own dark hair which he was twisting around one finger to help him keep concentrating on the complicated things his father was saying, but it was obvious that was not what his father meant. In his other hand he held the clay tablet and said so.

"Just show Gabael that tablet then," Tobit said. "He is a good businessman and will see immediately that it has both our marks on it. I mean his mark and mine. Then one thing will follow another as easily as falling out of bed."

To his horror Tobias discovered that the young woman had crept into the kitchen while they were laying their plans and was standing so close that he could feel her warm breath on the back of his neck.

"Well," he said, "I will do the best that I can."

FOUR

Enter the Archangel

Tobias was not a fool although in moments of exasperation his father sometimes treated him like one. When he was slow to respond to what was happening around him, it was not because there was something wrong with him the way some people believed but usually just because he was occupied with other matters. Absentminded is a far better term for him than softheaded. Much of the time his mind was simply absent somewhere else.

When Tobit was giving him instructions about the trip to Media, for instance, which was not nearly so far away as the boy thought although not exactly next door either, it was not the trip he was thinking about and most of the time not even the blue scarf. It was instead the bundles of dried herbs that were suspended from the ceiling directly above him and the way they looked to him like bushy-haired little men hanging by their heels. He wondered what it would feel like to be hanging up there beside them with all the blood going to his head and seeing everything upside down.

When he made the long walk to the palace to collect the court ladies' clothes for his mother, he was apt to have a vague smile on his face and even sometimes to lose his way, which served to confirm some people in their suspicion that he was a simpleton. The truth of it was that he was thinking about the invisible track that his feet were making as he wended his way through the crooked streets down to the Tigris and back again through still other crooked streets. He was thinking about how if you could only see this track, it would look like some sort of crazy, zigzagging loop and how if you could somehow put it together with all the other loops he had made going to all the other places he had gone to in his life, what an astonishing tangle you would end up with. No wonder he smiled.

Sometimes on his travels he would come across the king riding by in one of his armored chariots drawn by horses with braided manes or taking his ease on one of the palace terraces surrounded by slaves bearing ostrich-plume fans and by half-naked women. Then, if he was not careful, he would put his life itself in jeopardy by neglecting to prostrate himself on the ground as was the custom. Instead, he would stand there like a man in a trance thinking about how despite all the atrocious things they were always doing, like capturing and abducting his own people, the Jews, kings were only men very much like himself when all was said and done. They worried themselves sick when someone they loved was in trouble. They kept dogs. They stubbed their toes on the way to make water in the dark.

More often than not, the half-naked women would set him not so much to desiring them as to dreaming about the mystery of nakedness in general and how the Jews were so intent on hiding theirs from each other that even in the privacy of their own houses, they went about swathed from head to toe in shirts that hung to their ankles and shawls that went over their shoulders and hats that were pulled down low on their brows. All you could see of the women as they went about their errands in the streets was the glint of their eyes looking out at you over their veils. Men and women alike, it was as if their bare bodies caused them such shame that they preferred to move about the world looking like badly wrapped parcels rather than give anyone a glimpse of them. Tobias, on the other hand, thought of his own bare body as the most valuable possession he had and considered that part of it that was deemed most shameful to be the most entertaining of all because of how it seemed to have a life entirely of its own and to be forever reminding him in various comic ways of its presence even at moments when he had more or less forgotten that it existed.

When Tobit gathered him and his mother for prayers with the special shawl draped over his head and the special lamp flickering on the kitchen table, Tobias often stopped praying altogether because he was so busy thinking instead about whom he was praying to. His father told him again and again how careful he must be because the eye of the Holy One was always upon him and the score constantly being kept, and that was why, before he knew what he was about, the boy would often forget all the words of the prayers he was supposed to be repeating and meditate instead on the mystery of scorekeeping. In games like stick-and-ball or dice or mumblety-peg, just as in sports like racing along the bank of the river or wrestling or throwing the pole, to keep score meant to keep track of who won and who lost. But in your life itself, which Tobit claimed that the Holy One, blessed be he, was always watching with closest attention, how were you supposed to tell whether you were winning or losing, or how you were supposed to play it right, or even what the rules of such a complicated game were, when even as his father was urging him to do good deeds, his mother was pointing out that it was precisely his father's good deeds that had brought about their ruin?

What his father was urging him to do now, however, was to go to Media, and it was bearing down on him so relentlessly that for once he made a real effort to keep his mind from wandering off into the clouds even though that was more his inclination than ever because the trip seemed much too complicated to think about. It would be complicated enough just to find his way to a distant kingdom and then within that kingdom to a particular city and within that city to a particular house where he was expected to persuade a man who didn't know him from Adam to hand over two bags of silver worth a king's ransom. But on the morning after Tobit first broached the matter to him, he added another charge that made it more complicated still.

"It would be nice," Tobit said, "if somewhere along the way you could find yourself a wife."

They were finishing their breakfast while Anna worked at her loom in another room, and he made the remark in such a seemingly casual way that at first it seemed to Tobias that he was asking no more than for him to pick up a basket or two of pistachio nuts if he happened to come across any on his travels, and for a moment the boy took it just as casually. It mightn't be so bad to have a wife, he thought, if his eye happened to light on one that caught his fancy. But as Tobit pursued the subject further, he began to feel a knot in his stomach.

"I don't expect to be around much longer," Tobit said, "and it would brighten considerably what days I have left if you would get yourself married before I go. I will never live to see grandchildren, of that I am sure, but I would enjoy going to my grave knowing that I stand at least a chance of having a few someday."

In other words, Tobias realized, there was a deadline he

was supposed to meet, and the knot in his stomach tightened. At the thought of having children, it grew tighter still.

"You understand, of course, that not just any wife will do," his father went on, and there was nothing casual at all in the way he fixed his milky eyes on him across the table. It was hard to believe that he was not actually seeing him. "She can't be a Mede or a Babylonian or anything of that sort not only because the law of our people forbids it but because if I weren't dead already, it would be the death of me to see descendants of mine running around the streets with foreign blood in their veins. It would be the straw that breaks the camel's back if the camel's back hadn't been broken long since."

Tobias felt an almost irresistible temptation to escape the conversation into cloudy thoughts about camels such as the unforgettable smell of their urine and the piteous wail of the mothers when their calves were taken from them, but at the same time he felt such a surge of pity for his father, who for all he knew might be right about being at death's door, that he forced himself to pay attention.

"Noah and Abraham and Isaac and Jacob," Tobit said, ticking them off on his fingers. "Every last one of them chose wives from their own tribe. So don't you go falling for some high-stepping half-breed with a ring in her nose."

Anna occasionally wore a small gold ring in her nose, and Tobias's lips parted in a smile that was instantly erased by his father's final words on the disturbing subject.

"Don't let the grass grow under your feet," he said, knocking over his cup of wine as he groped for another ash cake. "By this time tomorrow at the latest I want you on your way. Find yourself somebody who knows the roads to go with you, and I'll pay whatever it costs."

So great was his father's vehemence that even before the wine was dry on his clothes, Tobias found himself out on the streets wondering not only how on earth he was going to accomplish all that was asked of him but where on earth he should start.

It was by a fishmonger's stall in the market that I first approached him. The dog saw instantly through my disguise. He flattened himself out on his front paws with his chest on the ground and his neck arched upward so he could see into my eyes. What I saw in his was as gracious a prayer as any I have ever set down at the feet of Glory. He asked nothing for himself or for any of his four-footed kind but only that all should be well with his master. Though his chin was in the dust, his lean rump was at about the level of my knees, and I reached down and patted it.

Around one shoulder I had strung a sack in which there were several rolled up maps that were clearly visible from the way I had placed them. Among them were various other kinds of traveling equipment like forked sticks for snakes and traps for small game, and I held in my hand a tall staff with a hook at the top with a water skin dangling from it.

"What is the dog's name?" I asked, and because he had

never been given one, Tobias just shook his head vaguely for an answer. In order to get a better look at me, he came around the corner of the stall where the scales of the fish were glittering in the sun.

How can I put into the language of men what the dog had seen when he had taken his look? A forked fire? A gathering of light that is always moving and always still? A pair of wings such as a dream might wear if the dream were a bird? Something like that anyway, or nothing at all like that. He saw the prayer carrier anyway. He saw Raphael.

What Tobias saw was a man only a little older than himself with a pedant's sharp nose and small, horizon-scanning eyes. Bound around his ankles were a pair of boots cobbled out of ox-hide with soles thicker than a man's hand for tramping the rough surfaces of the earth. He also of course noticed the rolled-up maps and the traveling staff.

"Is it possible," he asked, "that you might be familiar with the city of Rages in Media? I haven't the faintest idea where it is myself except that it's farther away than the farthest place I have ever been to in my life, which isn't really all that far when you get right down to it."

The fishmonger was calling out his wares in such a deafening voice that we moved a few paces away to a pepper tree where the dog lay down in the shade with his ribs heaving like a bellows because of his excitement at my presence and the growing heat of the day.

"It is odd you should ask," I said, "because I have been to

Rages on numerous occasions and know all the roads to it like the back of my hand. It seems only yesterday that I spent some time there with one of our people by the name of Gabael."

For a moment or two Tobias said nothing as he marveled at this unforeseen stroke of luck. He drew a circle in the earth with the toe of one sandal and rubbed at his jaw which he kept clean-shaven instead of bearded like most of his people because beards had always struck him as yet another way they had of hiding their bodies from each other.

"I know how sudden and foolish this sounds," he said, "but I wonder if you might consider going there with me?"

This time I paused for a few moments myself so that too quick a response wouldn't put him on guard.

"I see no reason why not," I said after a bit. "I was planning to head in more or less that direction anyhow, and I'd welcome having somebody to talk to on the way."

The smile of the boy as he took my words in was as winning as a girl's although his face was a manly one even without a beard to make it seem more so.

"I must go talk to my father," he said, " but I will be back before you know it. Perhaps you will have a sherbet at my expense, and I'll leave you the dog for company."

Tobit was as delighted as he was surprised when the boy returned so unexpectedly soon with the news of his chance meeting, and he told him to go fetch the man, whoever he might be, as quickly as he possibly could so he wouldn't have time to change his mind. He wanted to ask him a few questions, he said, and there was also the matter of arranging a wage for his services that would be acceptable to them both. What followed was an interview of almost unparalleled tediousness because Tobit got off on the subject of ancestry, which the Jews have always found fascinating beyond all else.

The first question he put to me was what tribe did I belong to and what family within that tribe, and at the risk of having him angrily call off the whole arrangement his son and I had all but agreed to, I answered it with a question of my own.

"Are you looking for a family tree," I asked, "or are you looking for someone to guide your son on a journey that it would be sheerest folly for him to undertake on his own?"

"I am looking," Tobit said, "for a man I can trust. Only a fool would trust somebody whose name and lineage he didn't know."

Because of the heat, it was one of the few times that he had left the house since his blinding, and the three of us met in the courtyard in the shadow of the wall, Tobias and I leaning up against it as we sat on the sparrow-spattered earth and Tobit on an overturned rain barrel facing us.

"My name is Azarias," I said, picking it out of the air, which is continually afloat with answers to even the prayers people haven't the wit to pray. They are always swarming all about them like midges over a pond.

"Ananias was my father," I said. "Perhaps you will remember that he was by no means the least illustrious of your relatives."

"Remember!" Tobit said, almost tipping over the barrel in his excitement. "And don't I remember too his distinguished brother Jathan, not to mention the esteemed Shemaiah, who was their father?" Then he was off and away into the fathers of fathers as many as seven generations back and which was the brother or husband of whom and so on and so forth. That was only part of it.

He remembered as well, he said, how before the Assyrians had carried their people off into captivity, he and the man I had so fortuitously thought to name as my father used to journey south to Jerusalem together. Shoulder to shoulder they had worshiped there in Solomon's great temple, which made even the palaces of Nineveh look sick by comparison. Side by side they had offered the firstborn of their flocks at the altar and the tenth part of all their vegetables and grain while most of their compatriots in the Northern Kingdom only laughed at what seemed to them a foolish excess of piety. You could tell from his face that Tobit was seeing their faithlessness in such vivid detail that it was as if his sight had been miraculously restored, and as he sat there fulminating against them, punctuating each new attack with a thump of his fist on the barrel, you could tell too that he had all but forgotten the business at hand and would have continued his diatribe indefinitely if I had not interrupted him by rattling my traps and forked sticks.

"Well, you come from good stock, there's no question about that," he said after pausing long enough to remember who I was and why I was there. "There remains now only the question of money."

He had turned his eyes in what he thought was my direction but was actually looking straight at Tobias, who frowned uncomfortably at the thought that maybe his father was expecting him to be the one to deal with so delicate a matter.

"I am prepared to offer you a drachma a day for as long as it takes," he said.

From the little nod of Tobias's head I knew that the offer was a fair one, but in keeping with my role as Azarias, I heaved a melancholy sigh and rose to my feet as noisily as I could to make him think I was leaving.

"Plus expenses, of course," he said. "That goes without saying."

"All right then," I said. "I'm not one to haggle with a kinsman."

To my surprise then, I saw that though his eyes were otherwise useless, they could still fill with tears. With the bargain struck, he knew at last that the journey would be made and the silver retrieved which would be more than enough to support his wife and his son for the rest of their days in comfort after he had gone to his grave as he expected to do at any moment in keeping with the prayer he had prayed on the day when Anna had refused to return the goat and insulted him.

Anna's tears came later. Tobias and I had gone back to the market to fit him out with boots and a staff like mine and to buy food for the journey and such other equipment as might come in handy on our way including a pole and hooks for fishing.

"Why are you sending him off on a wild goose chase like this?" she said as she packed two extra shirts in a bag for him with some dried figs, several seed cakes, and a phial of powdered herbs in case he was taken sick on the road. "What will we have left after the boy is gone? Can you imagine what this house will be like without the sound of his big feet clattering on the floor and that ridiculous whistle he makes through his teeth for calling the dog? Have you never stopped to consider that he is the mortar that holds our lives together and the bright star in our sky?"

In emulation of the court ladies whom she admired as much for their elegance as she deplored them for their supercilious ways, she had taken to painting around her eyes with kohl, and it had started to run down her cheeks along with the tears.

"And all for the sake of money," she said. "We have money enough and to spare thanks to my earnings. Don't you see that money is dung compared with our only son? As surely as I know my right hand from my left, I know that something awful is going to happen to him. We will never see him again."

I feel I have done Anna an injustice up to now in my description of her. It is true that she could be overbearing and sometimes had a sharp and wounding tongue. When they were quarreling over the goat, she should never have told Tobit that he understood as little of the world as his eyes could see of it and that his ill-advised charities had brought about their ruin. It is true too that she did preposterous things with her hair and was not above rapping her husband on the head with a wooden spoon when a dark mood was upon her. But at the same time she was a faithful and hardworking wife and mother, and her heart was at bottom no less tender for the way she kept it most of the time hidden. She truly loved Tobias, and her tears at the thought of losing him forever were by no means unmixed with tears also for Tobit because she knew how he loved the boy too and would live to regret having sent him to his doom.

Tobit felt his way to where she was bent over the bag she was packing and laid his hand on her shoulder. His look of perpetual surprise became surprise at how deeply he found himself sorry for her.

"Don't worry, my sister," he said, drawing her to him. "The boy will come back safe and sound, you will see. Everything will work out for the best." And when this didn't seem to comfort her much, he added one further word. "The Holy One, blessed be he, will send a good angel to attend him."

He said it to ease her grief without for one moment thinking it was true. Like most of his people most of the time, he could not find it in his heart to believe that the Holy One would be bothered to do any such thing even if it happened to occur to him and he happened to have an angel to spare for such a trivial errand. He also would never have dreamed that the Holy One might feel as sorry for them both as he himself felt for Anna.

But he could tell from the feel of her shoulder that what he said had at least stopped her weeping.

FIVE

The Fish

WE HAD PUT MANY DAYS AND MILES BEHIND US WHEN WE camped for the night by the river Tigris. Up a bit from the bank there was a grassy slope with daffodils growing here and there and a tamarisk tree with a wide-spreading crown of branches for shelter. A bend in the river had made a pool with a sandy shore where a few long-legged birds were stalking about through the reeds. The water looked cool and dark, and because it was still a hot day, although the sun was already low on the horizon, and because we were both of us footsore from the long way we had traveled, Tobias decided to go for a swim while I remained on the bank with my fish pole hoping to catch our dinner.

He untied his boots from his ankles, laid out his damp shirt and drawers on the grass to dry, hung his broad-brimmed straw hat from one of the tamarisk's lower branches, and waded into the pond up to his knees where he stood as naked as birth with the golden light of late afternoon upon him. No other Jew in all Nineveh would have dreamed of committing such an indecency with the eye of another upon him, but it was clear from the way he threw back his head and opened his mouth to the sky as he splashed water on his chest and arms that it bothered him not a whit. He knew that in youth even the bodies of men can be pleasing to the eye, and if others thought differently, so much the worse for them. What he did not know was that deep in the pond there lived an extraordinary fish.

What manner of fish it was I cannot say because whatever markings might once have identified it had long since been obscured by all the years it had spent growing to roughly the size and shape of the Egyptian woman who had summoned up Asmodeus. Its eyes were not the usual moon eyes of a fish but small like a pig's. It was covered all over with patches of moss and bleary, long weeds that trailed behind as it made its way slower than time through the water. The color of it was more like mud than anything else except for some splotches here and there that glinted like tarnished silver. Its stubby fins seemed inadequate to the task of piloting such bulk, and there was a thicket of whiskers about its lips. Its mouth was enormous. When opened as wide as it would go, it made it seem less a fish with an enormous mouth than an enormous mouth with fins and a tail to propel it.

For reasons known only to the Holy One, it is not given to fishes to speak, but part of the use it found for its mouth was, in cascades of bubbles and windy gasps, constantly to sing wordless praises of the pond, of the mud, the weeds, the darkness and coolness, and indeed of the whole creation itself as far as the fish was aware of it. The other use of its mouth was to eat. It rejoiced so in everything that it wanted to devour everything. Other fish, the dangling roots of lilies or legs of birds, a fisherman's boots or hat or oars or whatever might happen to fall into the water, possibly even a fisherman's boat, the fish gobbled up to the glory of God.

And then came the moment when it happened to swivel its eyes a bit to one side and caught sight of Tobias. With the force of one of the winged bulls of Nineveh, it hurled itself out of the water and would doubtless have swallowed him whole if I hadn't shouted to him from the bank to catch it by the leathery gills and wrestle it onto the shore. Luckily the young man's strength was equal to the task, and once we had cut it open and removed its heart, liver, and gall, which I directed him to put aside for safekeeping, we roasted it over a fire and ate as much of it as we could among the daffodils while the sun turned the sky to crimson.

"Azarias," he said as we lay looking up at the stars through the tamarisk branches waiting for sleep, "what on earth do you plan to do with that awful mess you said we should save? Maybe the dog would like it, though I have my doubts."

The dog gave a single flop of his tail and then rolled over to show us his back as a way of responding to his master's suggestion.

"The heart and liver are one thing and the gall another," I said. The moon had turned the eyes of the boy to silver, and thinking the silver lids might fall unless I spoke quickly, I told him all in one breath that the heart and liver, if burned, made a smoke that would drive off demons, and that a poultice made of the gall was useful in treating diseases of the eye. I could have spared myself the trouble, however, because before the words were out of my mouth, he gave a short snore and rolled over to lie on his side with his cheek on his folded hands.

SIX

The Towers of Ecbatana

It WAS NOT UNTIL MANY MILES AND DAYS LATER THAT WE CAME at last to within sight of the city of Ecbatana, where the Medes who could afford it gathered in large numbers every year to escape the summer's heat. They lived in terraced houses with tiled roofs and sweeping views of the mountains that rose all about them like the waves of a tumultuous sea. They bathed in streams that even with the sun at its hottest remained so chill from the melting snow that it was almost beyond endurance and rubbed shoulders with all manner of people such as Babylonian astronomers, Phoenician admirals, and Greek courtesans and physicians, all of whom were there to take their ease like them and to spend their money on such fripperies as chests of fragrant cedar from the groves of Lebanon and every imaginable kind of bauble put together with ivory from Ethiopia, gold from Sardis, turquoise from Egypt, and so forth.

The towers of the city could already be seen rising above the mist-filled valley which our road wound through, and we stopped for a meager lunch of what little was left of our provisions. Tobias was tanned as a camel driver from our weeks of travel, and he had long since given up wearing his boots which he said pinched his feet and raised blisters, hanging them instead about his neck by their long laces. His straw hat had been gnawed to pieces by mole rats one night while we slept so he had taken to tying around his brow like a pirate the blue scarf that had been given him as we left by the young woman whose warm breath he had felt on the back of his neck while his father was talking. Even the dog looked travel-worn. He slouched along with his nose almost touching the ground and his tail no longer arched over his roach back like a pennant but sagging dejectedly between his feathery shanks.

"That's Ecbatana," I said, pointing at it with the haunch of a rabbit we had roasted the day before. "Generally speaking, it's a place for a young man like yourself to steer clear of because it is full of frivolous people who would do you no good."

I said this in the character of Azarias despite the fact that in truth there was much there that struck me as charming, and the Holy One too if I may presume so far. Frivolous they might be, but the people of Ecbatana at least saw that the world was created for their delight, and as they jumped about in the frigid streams and wasted their money in the crowded bazaars, they came closer to living their lives as the Holy One intended than those who were continually apologizing for their unworthiness and trying to avert the wrath of the One who, had they but known, wishes the world only well.

"All the same," I went on, "we will sleep there tonight in the house of a man named Raguel. He is an acquaintance of mine and I've no doubt also some sort of relative of yours since one way or another all Jews seem to be related if you go back far enough as they do at the drop of a hat."

"The name rings a bell," Tobias said. He had stretched out in the sun with the blue scarf shielding his eyes and his arms flung out far to either side on the grass. "I think I have heard somebody mention him."

"Nothing would surprise me less," I said. "He is well known for many things, not the least of which is his daughter, Sarah."

"Sarah . . . Sarah . . . ," Tobias mumbled in a puzzled way as if the name was part of a dream he couldn't quite remember or hadn't quite finished dreaming.

"She is very beautiful and also very enterprising, a rare thing in women," I said, again almost biting my tongue as I said it because by and large I have found women more enterprising than men and spoke as I did only for the sake of sounding like Azarias.

"Beautiful?" Tobias said, lifting one corner of the scarf as if I might somehow produce her for him to see with that one bright eye.

"There are trees that resemble her a little," I said. "Slender trees on the order of willows, with long leaves that fall about them cool and green like a girl's long hair."

"I have seen girls like that," Tobias said. "They're scarce as hen's teeth in Nineveh though."

"And everywhere else too," I said. "They are worth more than their weight in gold because the fact of the matter is that they weigh very little, with their thin waists and delicate young bodies."

"Delicate and young. Like a willow," Tobias said, pulling the scarf back over his eye as if hoping to reenter the dream he had been dreaming.

"All of which leads me to the subject of marriage," I said, and at the word "marriage" the boy sat bolt upright in the grass with his eyes no longer sleepy and vague but wide as a deer's at the approach of hunters.

"Perhaps you will remember what your father told you," I said. "Unless I'm mistaken, he said that he hoped beyond all things that, like Abraham, Isaac, and Jacob before you, you would choose a wife from among your own people, a nice Jewish girl with a family background as respectable as your own."

Tobias had taken the scarf in his hands and was twisting it up into a series of knots and then untwisting them as he listened.

"What I propose to do on your behalf and with your approval, of course," I said, "is to open negotiations with Raguel for her hand when we stay under his roof this very night."

Tobias was on his feet now, standing beneath the blue sky with the mountains behind him and the distant towers. He kept thumping his forehead with the heel of his hand as if to dislodge some elusive memory or anything else that might serve as an escape from so unsettling a conversation. Sensing his discomfort, the dog had raised his head to look at him, panting with all his back teeth showing and saliva dripping off the end of his tongue.

"Raguel," he said. "Sarah. What is there about those names?" And then all at once his face went pale beneath his tan, and he sank down on the grass again where the dog shambled over to him and placed one oversized paw in his lap.

"I have it," he said, and before he had a chance to explain, I knew of course what he had.

"She's married lots of husbands already," he went on in the slow, halting way of a man trying to recapture a dream at breakfast. "Four or five of them at least, maybe as many as seven. It was my father who told me. Something perfectly awful happened." I could see in his face that it was all flooding back on him at once, and he spoke in a hushed voice as though it was happening before his eyes. "Every single time a demon turned up in the bridal chamber. He had the teeth of a lion and a scorpion's sting for a tail. He wanted the girl for himself and didn't want anybody else to have her. One after the other, he attacked each of her husbands. And the next morning they carried them out feet first."

"You mustn't let it bother you," I said. "I'm being paid a drachma a day to take care of things, and I'll make sure you're absolutely safe."

"I'm not thinking just about myself, though that's bad enough," he said. "The demon scares me out of my wits, and I'd hate like anything to die with my throat ripped out by those teeth or foaming at the mouth from the poisoned sting. But I'm thinking about my father too, who has troubles enough as it is, being blind and everything. To lose his only child would probably be the end of him. I wouldn't be surprised if it was the end of my mother too though she's tougher than he is, and who on earth will be left to give them decent funerals once I'm gone?"

Tears had come into his eyes as he talked about his parents, but instead of wiping them away as unmanly the way others would have done in his place, he unashamedly let them slip down his cheeks.

"Listen," I said. "You remember the fish, don't you?"

At mention of the fish, his face returned to its normal color.

"It must have weighed a ton," he said. "I had all I could do and then some to haul it ashore."

"Then you will remember also how we kept some of its insides after we cleaned it."

"They still stink to high heaven," he said. "The dog almost throws up whenever he gets a whiff."

"Never mind about that," I said. "They will save the day for you even so, as you will see."

"They truly will?"

"Your wedding day," I said, "or maybe I should say your wedding night. When you enter the bridal chamber with your young bride, I will have given you certain parts of those insides to take into it with you. I will also give you instructions as to just what to do with them, and if you follow those instructions to the letter, the demon will be out of there forever in about two seconds flat. Then you and Sarah will live happily ever after, and she will bear you children, and your father and mother will be happy too for the rest of their days."

"She will bear me children?" he asked.

When I nodded in answer, his face went all soft and helpless, and I knew that the marriage would take place. I believe it was just at that moment, as he thought about how she would bear him children, that even before he set eyes on her beauty, he knew he would love her. I suspect that he would have loved her even if she had not been beautiful.

SEVEN

The Contract Signed

Raguel was a shy man who spoke very little, and Edna, his wife, was a bold woman who once she got started would go on and on until the person she was speaking to suddenly remembered an appointment that had to be kept or windows that should be shuttered in case of rain or children at home who needed to be fed. Although he was of a child's stature himself, standing scarcely as high as his wife's armpit, Raguel was given to the deep thoughts and strong feelings of a man although he rarely got the chance to express them. Edna, on the other hand, had a woman's wiry, energetic body, but inside that body was, as I have said, an uneasy child forever trying to convince no one more than herself that she was clever and grown up. But all in all they got along surprisingly well.

Raguel had learned over the years how to turn off his ears and give his mind to other matters during his wife's longer soliloquies. He also admired her forcefulness in difficult situations where his own inclination was to go hide under a bed. Edna, in turn, respected her husband's good judgment and the quiet way he had, on those occasions when he was able to get a word in edgewise, to make people listen to him with a degree of interest and respect that she felt was never shown her. But the greatest bond between them was that they were both unbelievers.

It was not that they believed necessarily that the Holy One didn't exist. They took the position that maybe he did and maybe he didn't and were more than willing to leave the final say-so to professionals such as the elders of their own people who could recite from memory the entire law of the prophet Moses, or to the Babylonian soothsayers and Egyptian priests and Median mages who could read the answer to virtually any question in the movement of the stars. As far as Raguel and Edna were concerned, even if it could be proved conclusively that the Holy One was indeed enthroned somewhere in the clouds the way it was claimed, they felt that it would make no more difference to them than if it could be proved conclusively that there was indeed a blue camel with seventeen legs living somewhere in the desert.

What they didn't for a moment believe was that the Holy One gave a tinker's dam for the world he was said to have created. If the prayers of the faithful ever reached him at all, he seemed to them to pay about as much attention to them as he would have paid to the chalky droppings of sparrows or to a sneeze. He looked with equal indifference on the just and the unjust and no more rewarded the good and chastised the wicked than he would have picked sides in a dog fight. The constant songs of praise and entreaty that rose to his ears from the temple in Jerusalem and similar places bored him to distraction, as did also the acrid smoke from the burnt offerings and the gurgling cries of unblemished lambs and bullocks whose throats were being slit by gory-fisted priests at the altar. If seven men died on their wedding nights under ambiguous circumstances and the rumor went round that maybe it was a demon who had done it or maybe it was the young bride herself, what could possibly have concerned him less? What was it to him that there wasn't a man in all Ecbatana who so much as dared dream of being the eighth to enter that fatal chamber no matter how generous a dowry might be involved because Raguel was canny and known to be prosperous?

It was with all these difficulties, of course, that their unbelief had started. Neighbors looked the other way when they saw Sarah coming at them down the street and pulled their children into doorways for fear her eye might fall upon them. When Raguel and Edna themselves showed up at some communal feast or patriotic jamboree, they invariably found that they were the only ones at their table, and if they happened upon a group of people they had known all their lives, everybody suddenly stopped talking.

Needless to say, they spoke of their unbelief to nobody. They weren't fools. If the subject of religion came up, even Edna held her tongue, and Raguel would gaze off into empty space as though he was thinking of something else. They rarely spoke about it to each other either, but each knew what was on the other's mind even so, and their very silence on the subject became as much what bound them together as the daughter whom they equally loved and worried about.

Nothing escapes the eye of the Holy One, of course. The whimper of a child in the dark rings as clear in his ears as the trumpets of battle, and if a man were to journey to the outermost fringes of the earth, even there would his eye be upon him. There are times when I suspect that he has appointed me to bring prayers to him simply for the sake of giving me something to do with my wings and that he knows every prayerful thought that ever wells up in a human heart even before it is spoken or if it is never spoken at all. Surely he knew also that Raguel and Edna had long since written him off, and why they had too, but unless I miss my guess, he didn't for a moment hold it against them. I would go so far as to say that it may even have caused him to think the more highly of them because their unbelief grew from a far more honest view of the wretchedness of things than the belief of the devout who see only what they choose to see and turn a blind eye on the rest.

And they were basically good-hearted as well. They didn't go around taking scraps from their plates and their cast-off clothes to the poor like Tobit, but Raguel never let his daughter's misfortunes embitter him or keep him from lending a helping hand when it was needed, and Edna, despite her conviction that everybody disliked her and with good cause, was the soul of hospitality and did everything she could to make the rare guest feel at home and comfortable.

When Tobias and I, for instance, came knocking at her door toward the end of a trying afternoon during which she had been shamelessly overcharged for a lapis lazuli broach and cut dead by a poor relation she had once lent money to, she nevertheless bade us the warmest of welcomes even before she had the faintest idea who we were. She ordered the maid-servant who looked like a man to bring a basin of warm water for washing Tobias's large feet, and when she noticed that the sharp nose that I wore as Azarias was running and had turned pink as the result of some flying pollen I must have inhaled on the way, she insisted on fetching me a clean cloth and offering to wipe it herself. I thought she might make a fuss about the dog, whose hairy belly was dripping with mud from a puddle he had lain down in for coolness, but she only patted him on the head, asking to be told the name he had never been given, and didn't bat an eye when he stretched himself out with a sigh of gratitude on her best carpet.

When Raguel came in from the garden where he had been having a quiet cup of wine all by himself before supper, the first thing he did was exclaim to Edna how much the young man's looks reminded him of his cousin Tobit. To my eye, there was no resemblance at all between that lean young face and his father's with its plump little grape of a mouth, but to Raguel it seemed altogether remarkable, and for once he took the floor from his wife and plied us with questions. Who were our people, he asked, addressing himself chiefly to Tobias, and where had we come from?

"My father says we belong to the tribe of Naphtali, and he ought to know," Tobias replied, looking a little embarrassed at all the attention he was getting including the basin of warm water in which the maidservant was at that moment washing his feet with an unpleasant expression on her face.

"The place where we live is the famous city of Nineveh. We were taken there heaven knows how long ago by one of those kings with the fake beards and the half-naked women who follow them around like pet weasels, and we've been there ever since."

The fake beards and the half-naked women seemed to make little or no impression on Raguel compared with the mention of Nineveh.

"Can it be that you know a relative of mine there by the name of Tobit?" he asked with more interest than he had showed in anything for a long time.

"I know him all right," Tobias said and smiled partly at the direction the conversation was taking and partly because the maidservant was drying between his toes with a rough cloth and it made him feel ticklish and silly.

"I hope you will tell me next that he is alive and healthy," Raguel said.

"I'll make that next if you want me to," Tobias said. "He was certainly alive when we left him a few weeks ago anyhow, and as far as I know, he's fit as a fiddle except for one problem. But there's one other thing maybe I should tell you first."

By now he was clearly beginning to enjoy himself. He liked Raguel, and he liked how clean and cool his feet felt for the first time since his swim in the pond when the fish almost got him. He also, of course, liked the idea of seeing Raguel's eyes pop out of his head when he heard what he was going to tell him next.

"Tobit is my father," he said, "if you really want to know."

No one who knew Raguel, including his wife, would have ever predicted his response to this sudden revelation. No sooner were the words out of Tobias's mouth than what that usually reticent man did was spring out of his chair like a rabbit, kiss the boy square on the lips, and then burst into tears with the words, "Son of that noble and good man!"

There were yet more tears when Tobias recovered himself enough to say that the only thing wrong with his father's health was that he was blind, and at that disclosure Edna shed some tears of her own. Part of why both of them wept was that they considered this to be yet one further bit of evidence, as if any was needed, that the Holy One was perfectly willing to let a noble and good man go blind if that was how the dice came up. Assuming, they both would have silently added, that the Holy One existed.

The sounds of all this commotion reached Sarah, who was in her room brushing her hair, and she came quickly to see what had caused it. The dog was the first to see her enter, and his single welcoming bark alerted Tobias, who had rarely heard him bark at anything before. It was then, as he turned to find out what had occasioned such an outburst, that he saw Sarah for the first time himself. He thought about the willow tree I had spoken of with its cool, green leaves. He thought about the children she was going to bear him and hoped he would remember to give them names.

Edna insisted that we should stay for supper and went on at some length about the food she was planning to give us unless she changed her mind at the last minute for some reason, and what room we would sleep in that night, and why it was more desirable than other rooms she might have offered us, and who had stayed in it last, and what had become of them since. Raguel, in the meanwhile, slipped quietly out of the room and saw to the slaughtering of one of his rams that in due course was roasted and served up in a broth of leeks and ginger together with a bowl of his sweetest and rarest wine.

After we had glutted ourselves and were sitting there with our eyes glazed and fat on our chins while the big maid-servant and her birdlike partner cleared away the dishes, it was Tobias, to my surprise, who brought up the true purpose of our visit. With the blue scarf still tied under his chin for a napkin, he rapped on the table to draw our attention as if he was already husband and father and master of his own house.

"Azarias," he said, "wouldn't this be as good a time as any to tell them what you said this afternoon while we were eating what was left of the rabbit?"

So I did what he asked and laid the proposal out before Raguel as persuasively as I could. I spoke of the ties of kinship that already united the young pair through Tobit, and of the robust good health and cheerful disposition of the bride-groom together with the maidenly charms and current avail-ability of the bride. Even as I was speaking, I could see the emotions both of rapture and of fear at war in Raguel's face. As soon as I rested my case, it was the rapture he first gave voice to.

"There is nothing on earth any dearer to my heart than such a match as you propose," he said, raising his wine cup into the air with such enthusiasm that some of it spilled on the table. "By the venerable law of our fathers before us as well as by his own obvious qualifications, this fine young man clearly has every right to my daughter's hand, and I can tell by the look in her eyes that she has every intention of giving it to him with the greatest pleasure."

Actually, Sarah was looking down toward the table at the time so there was no way Raguel could see what was in her eyes, but after a brief pause, he went on anyway.

"However," he said, a shadow darkening his brow, "there is something else I must tell you," and I could see that it was only with the most extraordinary effort that Edna was able to restrain herself from clapping her hand over his mouth. He made no mention of Asmodeus but otherwise proceeded to give as accurate an account as he himself knew of the seven previous husbands and their untimely ends.

"But for the present," he said when his account had come to its tragic close, "let's all raise our cups together to the unmixed joy of this meeting if to nothing else."

It was plainly his generous way of leaving Tobias a way out of the whole arrangement if the risk seemed too high, but, again to my surprise, the young man broke in with uncharacteristic boldness.

"I won't touch another drop of that stuff till the business is settled," he said, and that is how it came to be settled that very same night.

The maidservants were sent to fetch a scroll and the appropriate implements. The contract was written out by Raguel with myself peering over his shoulder to check the legalities. Then he and Edna both set their seals upon it, and as soon as that was done, Raguel took Tobias with one hand and Sarah with the other and blessed them both in the name of the One in whom he did not believe for a minute. And thus they were wed because that was all there was to it in those days.

It was not until Edna came into Sarah's room later as she was preparing for bed that the young woman showed her true feelings at last by starting to weep. Not knowing that she was already more than a little in love with the demon, Edna interpreted her daughter's tears as arising from her fear for Tobias's safety and told her to be brave and to pray for deliverance to the selfsame One whom Edna believed in no more than her husband. She gave her a great deal of other useful advice before drowsiness got the better of her. Then to Sarah's ill-concealed relief she finally went off to bed.

As Tobias and I were lying side by side in ours, I could hear over his contented snoring another sound that as far as I could tell might be either the breeze in the branches of the mulberry trees outside or the rustling of an unusually large pair of transparent wings.

The Wedding Night

Raguel had caused the bridal chamber to be built several years earlier on the occasion of the first of his daughter's weddings. It stood in a grove of willows some little distance from the house with a tiled roof for coolness in summer and a single window that was too high to look either out of or into without something to stand on. Because of its melancholy associations, it had fallen into neglect since the seventh and last time it had been used, and both of the maidservants working as a team needed the better part of a day to restore it to some kind of order.

Cobwebs had to be swept out along with the spiders who had woven them and a good many mouse droppings. The bed had to be aired and made up with freshly scented sheets and a number of silken pillows. The floor had to be strewn with green rushes. Sweet-smelling herbs were gathered and hung from the rafters over the bed together with a bundle of mandrake roots to ensure fertility and several images of questionable taste that were supposed to serve the same purpose. The larger maidservant handled the heavier part of the work with the smaller one twittering over the lighter, and by the time they were done, they were both sweaty and exhausted and full of hostility, which was made only the worse by the constant presence of Edna, who supervised the entire operation down to the most trivial detail and never stopped criticizing their work the entire time with endless advice how to do it properly. Fortunately for Edna, all of this kept her so busy that she had little time to worry about whether or not the demon would show up again. As Azarias, I had assured them that everything was under control, and although I did not explain my reasons for being so confident, fearing that they might think them fanciful and inadequate, she decided to take me at my word and simply leave the whole matter to fate since, because of her unbelief, she knew of nowhere else to leave it.

But not so Raguel, whose nature was always to expect the worst. He was certain that Asmodeus would arrive yet again with the same catastrophic results, and from sad experience he knew that there was nothing on earth he could do to prevent it even if he were to persuade all his neighbors to stand guard with clubs and spears and any other weapon of destruction they could lay their hands on. Besides that, the last thing he wanted was to let them find out what was happening because then, when Tobias was carried out like the others, it would only confirm them in their belief that the whole family was under a curse and lead to their shunning them all the more fervently in the future. So with no Holy One to call on for help, he fretted himself into such a state that when it finally came time for him and his wife to escort the bridal pair to the chamber that had been so elaborately prepared for them, he was so sick with anxiety and had drunk so much sweet wine to strengthen his spirits that it was all he could to do to walk.

Sarah was little better off than her father for two reasons. One reason was that, like him, she was afraid Asmodeus would appear. The other reason was that she was afraid he would not.

If he appeared, then this personable young man, who had won the hearts of both the father she adored and the mother she put up with as best she could, would end up like all the others. To be sure, he had not won her own heart because she had already half given it elsewhere, but even so she had admired the manly way he had spoken up at dinner the night before and had taken pleasure in the way the blue scarf matched his eyes and set off his tan, and the last thing she wanted was to be the cause of his undoing.

If, on the other hand, Asmodeus did not appear, then she would not only feel abandoned but also would be forced to sacrifice her maidenhood to a husband whom, for all his engaging ways, she did not love.

Tobias spent the day trying to teach the dog how to sit up on his hindquarters. At the start he simply snapped his fingers over the dog's head to give him the idea, but when it seemed instead just to puzzle him, he went and found a piece of ram from the previous night and after first getting the dog to sit on his haunches with his front legs stiff and his front feet planted on the ground, he dangled it over his nose. This worked to the extent that the dog actually managed to sit straight for a moment or two with only his hindquarters remaining on the ground and his forepaws beating the air as he strained for the prize, but then he flopped down on all fours again, looking up at his master with his gentle, apologetic eyes.

It was at that point that I intervened with a suggestion. I told him that when the dog was up on his haunches, I would take hold of his stout tail and draw it out on the grass behind so that it would help give him balance. This proved to work like a charm, and the dog was as pleased as Tobias when he found that he could sit as straight and tall as Esarhaddon on his throne for as long as anybody wanted.

The reason that Tobias was able to give himself to such light-hearted pursuits instead of fretting like the others as the fateful hour drew near was that I had explained to him by then how everything was going to turn out for the best thanks to the entrails of the great fish, which he seemed to have more or less forgotten all about despite the fact that the bag containing them had spent the night with us in Edna's guest room and that age had by no means improved their smell. As long as he followed my instructions to the letter, I told him, the demon would be rendered helpless, and I opened the bag where I'd been carrying them all those weeks and explained exactly what he was to do.

"This thing is the gall, and I'll tell you about that when the time comes," I said, putting it back in the bag. "Both the heart and the liver are what you see now though I admit it's a little hard to tell one from the other at this point. They are what you will take with you tonight."

"Good grief," Tobias said, screwing up his face and turning his head to one side.

"You will also take with you this copper basin which you will fill with live ashes from the incense that Raguel is sure to have burning next to the bed for good luck."

"I thought at first you were going to ask me to wear it," Tobias said, and placed the basin on top of his head for a moment in an attempt to cheer himself up.

"This is serious business," I said, trying to keep on sounding as much like Azarias as possible. "As soon as Raguel and that impossible woman have gone back to the house and left the two of you by yourselves at last, Asmodeus will arrive as surely as dark will follow dusk. But don't let that throw you off. He will be as unsure of himself at first as you are because demons have their problems just like everybody else, and you will have plenty of time for what has to be done."

"I certainly hope so," Tobias said, and taking the dog's face between his palms, he tipped it toward him for reassurance.

"More than enough time," I said. "What you will do next is put this mess, as you once called it, into the basin of burning ashes. In a moment or two it will give off a thick, greenish smoke that will make the smell you are smelling now seem like the roses of Sharon by comparison."

"I have never smelled the roses of Sharon," Tobias said, releasing the face of the dog.

"That is a pity," I said, "but no matter. I suggest that you and the bride hold your breaths for as long as you can. By the time you can hold them no longer, the demon will have taken to his heels as surely as prayers rise to Heaven, and you will never have to see him again for as long as you both shall live."

"I hope that will be for another hundred years at least," Tobias said. "I also hope you know what you're talking about."

"It's far more important," I said, adopting Azarias's pedagogic manner yet again, "that *you* know what I'm talking about. If you have been paying close attention, I swear to you all will be well."

"You swear on your mother's grave?" Tobias said, and when I nodded yes even though I never had a mother but only the One who is father and mother of us all, he seemed for the first time to believe everything that I had told him and asked if now I wouldn't like to go out in the garden with him and help teach the dog.

It was there, with the heart and liver of the fish in another bag under his shirt, and the copper basin wrapped up like a wedding present, and the dog sitting tall as a king in a lamb's-wool beard, that Raguel and Edna eventually joined us with Sarah between them. They led the way to the grove of willows, and there, after tearfully kissing both Tobias and their daughter good-bye, they opened the bridal chamber door to admit them and then closed it behind them and left.

Asmodeus failed to arrive quite as soon as I had predicted, and there were a few awkward moments during which Tobias, not prepared for this interlude, tried standing on his tiptoes and on various bits of furniture to see if he could look out of the window. Sarah found a chair as far from the bed as possible and with one finger traced the stitching of her silk veil over and over again. Then suddenly, out of nowhere like the wind, Asmodeus was before them, and Sarah pressed her hand to her heart.

His hair, as long as a woman's, was gathered in a knot at his nape, and the teeth of his smile glistened white as the snows of Ararat. Slender and sharp as a blade, he stood for a few moments with his hands on his hips and his slippered feet wide apart on the rushes. Tobias jumped off the stool, which had proved just high enough to give him a glimpse through the window, and rushed to his bride.

Asmodeus did not so much as acknowledge his presence but reached out one long-fingered hand and, removing Sarah's veil, ran it through her hair like a comb. With his other hand he tipped her face toward him much as Tobias had done with the dog. She lowered her eyes before his gaze, he lowered his lips to her brow, and the longing and fearing and shadowy caring that passed between them then made the ashes of the incense next to the bed glow as crimson as the sun that just then was sinking behind the towers of Ecbatana.

They were so lost in each other's presence that neither of them noticed as Tobias shot away to fill the basin with some of the glowing ashes and then emptied the heart and liver upon them. By the time he returned with it, the smoke had already started to rise in a greenish cloud, and he shouted to Sarah to hold her breath as I had advised him. Then something happened which, not having foreseen it, I had failed to warn him about.

As the smoke reached his nostrils, Asmodeus sprang away from the copper basin and crouched down in a kind of knot on the floor with his face pressed tight to his thighs and his hands over the back of his neck and his ears as if burning pitch was raining upon him. Slowly then he uncoiled like a serpent uncoiling, and when this process finally got him to his feet, he was no longer a skinny young man with a flashing smile and a woman's hair but a creature with a golden carapace over his head and shoulders, and the teeth of a lion in his mouth, and a tail like a lobster's snapping open and shut behind him, and wings so wide that they reached from one wall to the other, vibrating up and down with the noise of chariots in battle.

He held out his talons toward Sarah, and she held out her hands toward him. Then as the cloud of smoke started to spread through the air and thin out enough for her to see through to the unimaginable transformation that had taken place, she threw her arms around Tobias and buried her face in his shirt. Whatever it was that the demon shouted, with his head arched back as far as the carapace would permit and his tongue darting in and out like an adder's, it was lost in the deafening clatter of his wings. In another instant he was gone.

Tobias and Sarah at last let out their breaths with two explosive gasps to find that the air was clear again and filled only with the scent of the herbs and the glowing incense. Tobias was holding his bride in his arms, and when she finally unburied her face from his shirt, the eyes she looked into were no longer the eyes of the young man her parents had foisted upon her but the eyes of the husband who had delivered her from an unspeakable horror.

They were both so undone by all this that they sank down onto the rushes and lay there side by side for some little time in utter silence without so much as their arms touching. Even when they both felt more or less themselves again, they still remained silent because neither of them could think what to say. They were both of them virgins, and they were both of them as tired as they had ever been in their lives, and they were both of them more than a little afraid.

Tobias was the first to speak. He was lying on his side, propped up on one elbow with his cheek resting against the heel of his hand. He was studying her face carefully as though he thought he might find the right words there. She at the same time was studying his.

"Maybe we ought to say a prayer or something," he suggested in a rather hesitant way with no idea what had put the thought into his head, considering that he had always found prayers rather boring when Tobit had conducted them at home, and then realized he couldn't for the life of him remember so much as one of them. Sarah showed her agreement with a nod of her head. She knew of her parents' unbelief, but as for herself, she neither believed nor otherwise. If Tobias wanted to pray, she would do the best she could to pray along with him in her heart. For all she knew, somebody might even be listening.

Tobias couldn't think what name to call the Holy One by, and he was no good at names under the best of circumstances, so he didn't call him anything at all but just spoke as though picking up a conversation that had been going on for a long time.

"I'm really not taking this woman," he said, "because I desire to lie in her arms, though the truth of the matter is that I'd rather lie in them than anywhere else in the whole world. I'm taking her because I liked her from the first moment I heard her name from Azarias and started thinking about how someday I was going to have children with her. So will you have mercy upon us both, whatever exactly that means? And please let us live for a very long time together under the same roof. And thank you."

Not sure whether Tobias expected her to add anything, Sarah said just "Amen," and then Tobias said that maybe the best thing they could do next was to go to bed and get a little sleep because it was already almost dark and he himself was half asleep already and imagined she must be too after all that had happened. With considerable relief, Sarah said she felt the same way, and within moments they were lying side by side again only this time they could not see each other because there was so little light left. They were both of them thinking their own thoughts.

What Tobias was thinking was that whatever was supposed to happen next, at least it wouldn't have to happen right then. Sarah was thinking how considerate he was not to try to force his attentions upon her when she had scarcely had time to collect her wits. She was also thinking about what those attentions might be like and wondering how long it would be before she found out for herself. But the room was very quiet and peaceful, and it wasn't long before they were both of them fast asleep, this time with their arms just touching.

That was how it came about that they failed to hear the strange grating and crunching and softly thudding sounds from among the willows outside. They were the sounds that Raguel was making as he dug a grave. Unlike his distant cousin Tobit, the digging of graves was not one of his specialties. In fact he had never dug one before in his life. When each of the seven sons-in-law had met his fate, he had hired a neighbor's boy to take care of that depressing detail for him.

But in this case secrecy was essential. He was entirely convinced that Tobias would be found cold and stiff in the morning, and under no circumstances did he want the neighbors to get wind of it. Therefore he had arisen in the middle of the night, which was in itself no great hardship since he hadn't been able to get a wink of sleep anyway, and dragged himself outdoors with his shovel and started to work. This way, when things fell out as he felt certain they would, he could simply shovel Tobias under and no one would have to be the wiser.

It was a long, arduous job what with only the moon to see by and a racking headache to boot thanks to all the wine he had drunk, but in time he ended up with a hole that he could only hope was approximately the right length and depth, stuck his shovel in the pile of loose earth that he had excavated, and then sat down on the pile himself for a few moments of reflection. It occurred to him that it would make much more sense to bury the boy right then and there under cover of darkness than to wait for daybreak when there might very well be neighbors snooping around as they frequently did, and so he decided that he had better make absolutely certain that the boy was dead as he felt he had every reason to believe that he was.

He did not feel up to taking a peek himself because he was on the brink of collapse already and feared that the added strain might push him over the edge. Instead, he returned to the house where Edna was asleep on her back with her mouth wide open as usual and shook her awake. It took him a little time to make everything clear to her, but when she finally understood what he had done, she congratulated him on his good judgment and foresight and said she would send the small, birdlike maidservant to discover the worst because she would be quieter about it than the other one who could not walk across the kitchen floor without making the cups on the shelves rattle.

The small woman was appalled at being given such a macabre assignment at that hour, but knowing perfectly well that she would get a sound slapping if she so much as put up an argument, she padded across the chill, damp grass in her nightdress with an oil lamp in her hand and set about doing as she had been told.

Keeping her thumb tight on the latch when she opened the door to the bridal chamber so there would be no click as it fell back in place, she peered into the darkness with the lamp held high in her free hand. It was hard to see anything very well in the shadows, but she could make out at least that there were two bodies in the bed. The question was whether they were both breathing, and for the life of her she couldn't figure how to find out without being discovered. By a lucky chance, even as she stood there in her bare feet wondering what on earth to do next, one of the bodies rolled over in its sleep and emitted a little riffle of a snore that was unmistakably that of a man. As if by way of confirmation, there was almost immediately a kind of antiphonal murmur from the other body, and thus she was able to go back to her mistress with the unexpected good news that both of the young people gave every indication of being alive and well. She was so pleased by her success and so gratified by the compliments of her mistress and by the tearful thanks of Raguel that she forgot about the single misstep she had made, which was that on her way out of the bridal chamber, she had forgotten to keep her thumb on the latch with the result that the click it made was enough to wake up Tobias, and Sarah too, who took it for only the clatter of willow branches outside their window.

They lay there in silence for a while, neither of them sure whether the other was still sleeping and not daring to move so much as a finger in case that was so. After a while, Tobias thought he could tell from the way she was breathing that Sarah must be just as awake as he was and with his heart pounding in his chest decided to take the risk and find out.

"Are you asleep?" he whispered, almost too softly for even himself to hear. Her answer was to reach out and touch his hand.

It was thus that they finally made their way into each other's arms at last, and so engrossing was all that they found there that they did not even notice the bitter mutterings of the larger of the two maidservants as she set about filling in the moonlit grave among the willows as Raguel had told her to.

Asmodeus in the meanwhile had fled to the land of Egypt where he sat between the paws of the sphinx with his terrifying head in his hands. He had shouted to the girl that he loved her, and she hadn't even heard.

NINE

The Two Sacks
and Gabael

THE FEASTING THAT FOLLOWED WENT ON FOR A FULL FOURTEEN days. There was no end to the eating and drinking and no end either to the grumbling of the two maidservants as well as of the three or four others who were especially hired for the occasion. Raguel invited everybody he could think of for miles around not only because his heart was overflowing with benevolence because of the many marvelous things that had happened, which almost made him wonder if possibly the Holy One existed after all, but also because he wanted all

Ecbatana to know that the family curse had been lifted and his daughter was married to a preeminently eligible husband whom any young woman in the city would have been more than delighted to claim for her own. Edna also was in seventh heaven because for the first time in her life she found people not edging away at her approach but actually seeking her out and patting her on the arm and offering to do things like peel onions for the feast in hope that maybe some of her good fortune might rub off on them.

All this hullabaloo was no more to Tobias's liking than finding himself the constant center of everyone's attention with all the men hanging on his every word and all the women hanging on his sleeve, and he slipped away with Sarah, who felt much as he did, as often as he politely could although he was greatly cheered when Raguel drew him aside one afternoon during a lull in the festivities and told him that once the fourteen days were over, he was planning to turn over to him one half of his entire fortune with the sworn promise of the other half as soon as he and Edna were no more.

The bridal chamber was so heaped with wedding presents that he and Sarah could scarcely weave their way to bed at night through the stacks of cedar chests of all sizes, the piles of sumptuous clothes and bedding, and the endless things from the bazaars such as gewgaws of ivory and beaten silver and turquoise and all that. There were picnics on the banks of the icy streams, and midnight revels by torchlight. There were excursions into the mountains where peasants seemed to appear out of nowhere to do abandoned dances in their honor.

It was somewhere around the eighth or ninth day that Tobias found me where I was sitting behind a large acacia tree in hopes of being granted a few moments' peace. There were circles under his eyes, and his shirt was torn where one of the dancing peasants had grabbed it in an excess of high spirits. For once the dog was not with him, probably because he was hiding one place or the other like me. Tobias squatted down on his heels and dabbed at his brow with the blue scarf which he still occasionally carried with him for old time's sake.

"I really don't know what I am going to do," he said in much the same way he had prayed on his wedding night as if simply picking up on a long-standing conversation. "Heaven only knows how many days we still have to keep on whooping it up with these lunatics, but it must be five anyway, maybe even six, and Raguel says there is no possible way I can leave till the whole thing's over without insulting all Ecbatana. Which might not be such a bad idea," he added, tucking the blue scarf back inside his shirt. "At least it would get them out of my hair."

In a moment or two he went off on a different tack. "Do you remember," he asked, "about those two sacks of silver I was supposed to bring home and about what's-his-name that I was supposed to get them from, and the clay tablet and all that? There has been so much going on that it completely slipped my mind."

I had rarely heard him speak in such long sentences before, I suppose because he was so weary that once he got going, he didn't have the energy to stop.

When I told him that I remembered, he started off again.

"I've been talking to Raguel," he said, "which isn't the easiest thing in the world to do because he's running around so fast keeping everybody's wine cup filled to the brim that it's almost impossible to catch him, and he says that if I want, he can let me have two camels and some flunky to drive them and the flunky can go in my place and get this man, whoever he is, to give him the silver and then bring it back here to me."

By now he had stretched himself out under the acacia tree and with one raised finger was counting the birds in its branches.

"My father says you have to trust people and not go around with the idea that every one of them is some kind of crook or out to sell you his sister, and I'm sure he's right, but I'm also sure even my father would think twice before expecting some unknown servant to handle the kind of money we're talking about without having some of it stick to his fingers."

"It's obvious what you're leading up to," I said, "and nothing would give me more pleasure than to get away from all this for a few days and go along myself to make sure the full amount is returned to you safely. Tell Raguel to make sure the camels are well watered. I'll be ready to leave at the drop of a hat."

"I count seven birds and something else that's either a bat or a mouse," he said, pointing at them one by one before finally returning to the subject.

"I don't know where I would be without you," he continued. "I wouldn't be here for one thing, and I wouldn't be married for another, and I wouldn't be eating and drinking myself into a fit every day and getting next to no sleep. When you stop to think about it, where I would probably be is the stomach of that awful fish, or lying six feet under with my throat torn out. When you come back with the silver, it would be nice if you could bring that man back too who's been keeping it all these years so at least I can tell Father I saw him as he asked me to. What was his name by the way?"

"His name is Gabael," I said, "and he lives in the city of Rages, which is not such a long journey from here as journeys go. He'll insist I spend the night with him because it would reflect badly on his hospitality if he did any less, but I should be back here well before it's time for us to go home even so."

"I hope so," Tobias said. "We've been gone for weeks now, and my parents will be absolutely sure I'm dead if I don't turn up soon."

"I will take care of everything," I said, and he tossed a bit of moss up into the tree, which scattered the birds.

"I hope this Gabael doesn't give you a hard time," Tobias said. "My father told me he put seals on the two sacks just to play it safe, and he made sure I took along the clay tablet with both their marks on it to prove they were his. It makes me wonder if he really trusts everybody as much as he says."

"It's just that he always expects that the worst of all possible things is the thing that's bound to happen because that's the way of it among you people," I said. "You forget that as often as not what happens is a very good thing. But never mind about that now. You can be sure Gabael will give me no trouble."

And he didn't. He turned out to look rather a good deal like the fish, with the same small, porcine eyes and gaping chasm of a mouth in a thicket of whiskers. He lived in a marble house with any number of wives ranging in age from eleven or so up to whatever he was himself. In the evening, before dinner, he had them bring in a great many of his children, who proceeded to sing every last verse of a few of the most tiresome songs that have ever been written. He also offered me the loan of any of the wives who happened to strike my fancy and suggested that since the clothes I was wearing looked shabby and travel-stained, he would consider it an honor if I would accept as a gift any that I might happen to choose from his own wardrobe. It was all I could do to prevent him from pressing on me then and there the tunic he was wearing, which was of Egyptian cotton dyed purple and sewn all over with pearls.

He didn't seem to remember Tobit at all when I spoke of him, saying only that the name was perhaps slightly familiar, but as soon as I brought up the subject of the two sealed sacks, he led me at once into a room with a grating at the single small window where a great many other sacks of assorted sizes were stored. He carefully examined the clay tablet I had brought and checked it for Tobit's mark as well as for his own. In no time then, he produced the sacks I was after. Despite all Tobit's and Tobias's misgivings, he turned them over to me with the most cordial of smiles, adding that if Tobit was still feeling pinched, he would be happy to let him have virtually anything more he might need at an unusually low rate of interest because of their former association.

He also said that he would be delighted to accept the invitation to return with me to the wedding feast and insisted I travel with him in his huge gilded wagon with iron-bound wheels which had belonged once to some warring Median king or another and which he had converted to the uses of peace by filling it with thick carpets and embroidered cushions and every imaginable delicacy to eat and wines of the greatest rarity to drink and a fringed canopy overhead, with side curtains, to protect us against the sun.

He created a sensation in Ecbatana. For a while even Tobias, much to his delight, was overshadowed by him. People clambered all over his wagon, sampling the food and poking at the upholstery and running their hands over the sleek necks of the six giant horses that pulled it. Two or three times every day he changed into a new costume with different jewels glittering in his turban and some new perfume in his thick, oily hair. His expansive manner and the way he had of putting his arm around the shoulders of whichever wedding guests he was talking to as though they were his oldest and most valued friends endeared him to everybody.

He made such a special fuss over Edna that, impossible as it was to imagine, I could only assume that he was after her for his harem. She was of course charmed off her feet by his gallantry and would unquestionably have followed him to the ends of the earth if she hadn't been so loyal to her husband. When Gabael sang songs to her, she colored like a girl. When he told jokes, her laughter almost threw her to the ground. When at the end of his visit he insisted on presenting Sarah with an emerald roughly the size of her fist and Tobias with a scimitar with a gold hilt and a scabbard of carved leather, she burst into tears of gratitude. He blessed the bridal pair then in the name of every god he could think of and not long afterwards rumbled off back to Rages in his wagon.

There were still two days left till the end of the feasting, and Tobias was more anxious about his parents than ever.

"They must be completely beside themselves by now," he said, and he was right.

Return to Nineveh

"He has probably just been held up for some reason," Tobit said to his wife. "A trip like that always takes longer than you think, and you have to expect delays. Maybe they followed the wrong road. Maybe the weather was against them. Who knows? Maybe they couldn't find Gabael's house or they found he'd moved away and had to look around for somebody else to give them the money."

"Our son is dead," Anna said. "A mother knows such things in her heart."

For some days she had done nothing about her hair, and it hung mouse-colored and uncombed about her shoulders. Her eyes were bleary with weeping, and there was no kohl around them. Several piles of the court ladies' laundry had sat for a week or more, unwashed and unmended, in a basket in the kitchen.

"O Tobias!" she said, waving her wooden spoon about in a distracted way, "Why did I ever let you go? You who were always the light of my eyes."

"Think about me," Tobit said. "I don't have any eyes."

This only made her feel worse, and she buried her face in her hands. She grieved for her husband. She grieved for herself. She pictured Tobias in the ditch in some godless land full of scoundrels and assassins. His throat had been slit, and the dog was on his haunches beside him with his hairy nose pointed skyward and his ears flat to his head. He was singing the most tragic song that a dog can sing.

"It's all in your mind," he said, feeling his way to the stove where she sat and patting her. "The boy is perfectly fine, I assure you. He'll be back any day now. There is absolutely no cause for worry."

"We will never set eyes upon him again," she said.

Nevertheless, every day she made her way to the north gate of Nineveh, which was the one that the boy would return by if he ever returned. It was guarded by two winged bulls with the curly beards and beehive-shaped crowns of a king. There was always a crowd gathered there—peddlers and immoral women and beggars squatting against the wall for shade with their ingratiating gestures and toothless patter. For hours on end Anna would wait in their midst with only her nose and eyes showing through the folds of her head cloth so that nobody would recognize her and try to strike up some pointless conversation. For hours on end she would watch the road for some glimpse far in the distance of the boy and the dog coming home.

Tobias pictured his parents' anxiety in his mind almost as clearly as if he had actually been there to see it. There were times when he forgot about it, to be sure, what with all the celebrations to occupy him, which grew more frenetic than ever with their end approaching, not to mention the nights when he and Sarah were finally able to escape to the cluttered bridal chamber where they forgot everything in the world except each other. But the thought of his parents kept returning like a toothache, and he started counting the hours until we could start back for Nineveh at long last.

Raguel was counting the hours too, though for other reasons. He dreaded the day when Sarah would leave more than he had ever dreaded anything before in his life. He thought of all the evenings they had enjoyed together when Edna was mercifully busy at some chore like taking an exhaustive inventory of the larder because she was convinced that the maidservants took things home, or making a list in her head of all the people who had treated her even more shabbily than usual so she could make a point of not speaking to them the next time they met.

Then Sarah and he would go off to the willow grove, perhaps, or find some secluded corner of the garden, and she would tell him what it was like to be growing up and he would tell her what it was like to be growing old. She would speak of the excitement of making new friends, who seemed as different and exciting to her as to her father they seemed very like all her other friends, and of learning new songs, which sounded to him exactly the same as the songs he had grown up with. She would speak of her hope that someday a handsome young man would come along to make her his wife and of the new life they would lead together, which her father could only hope would not eventually turn flat and stale like other lives he had observed.

He for his part would speak to her mainly of old times, especially of old times that they had shared. He spoke of how when she was a child they used to go to a hillside outside the city where there was a small pond that most of the year was warm enough for bathing and how he would sit in the shade and watch her paddling around in it in her drawers or trying to catch some of the moths that swarmed over it in a cloud toward the end of a summer afternoon. He spoke to her about how desperately worried he and Edna had been when at the age of ten or so she had for no apparent reason grown thin and pale, and how they had taken turns sitting up with her at night and bringing her warm milk to drink. He talked about the black pony they had given her with a star on its forehead, which he had taught her to ride on, and about games they used to play like beans-in-the-cup.

Remembering these things made him feel like a young man again, and he was afraid that once she was gone, he would change into an old one overnight with nobody left to talk to except Edna. Besides that, for years his conversations with his wife had been so centered on Sarah that once she was gone he couldn't imagine what they would find to talk about instead.

He mentioned none of this to Sarah, of course, not wanting to burden her with his troubles at such a festive time, but she knew perfectly well how he felt anyway. She looked forward with great excitement to going off with Tobias, whom every day she found more to her liking, but she knew what it would be like to look back in a few days at the short figure of her father standing in the doorway waving good-bye.

The closest they ever came to talking about this sadness they each of them felt and knew the other was feeling was on the next to the last day of the feasting when Edna was out on the street explaining in detail to Tobias and the servants just how they were to load the wedding presents into the carts and Raguel was in the bridal chamber helping Sarah pack the last of her things in a box. He found himself talking about religious matters for some reason. Ever since the arrival of Tobias and all the good things that had come about as a result, he said, he had been wondering if there was a God who looked after the world after all. He had seen so much evidence to the contrary, particularly those seven untimely deaths, that he had no intention of changing his views all in a minute, but these recent strokes of good luck had at least given him pause. It was beginning to be conceivable to him, he said, that the Holy

One was not as remote and indifferent as a blue camel with seventeen legs living in the desert but that he actually intervened in the lives of his people from time to their benefit. Hadn't Tobias come like a gift from Heaven? But at the same time, he went on, there were shadows that the Holy One seemed to have overlooked. He did not mention that for him the darkest shadow of all would descend upon him the next day when his child was to leave for good, taking his chief delight with her and leaving him and Edna to live out the rest of their lives together as best they could, but both he and Sarah knew what he was thinking about.

In spite of all this, he managed to put on a brave face and helped her fold her things and tuck them into the box neatly so there would be no wrinkles, and it was only when he was left to himself that he gave vent to his true feelings. Sarah had gone out to fetch something from the house that she had forgotten, and as he picked one of her shawls out of the box to smooth it flat and refold it, he suddenly found himself pressing it to his lips and allowing his tears to flow at last.

It was the next day, with their departure now only an hour or two away, that he made a desperate last move. He drew Tobias aside and offered a suggestion that even as he was offering it he knew would be almost certainly turned down.

"I know you are worried about your parents," he said, because Tobias had said that he was, "and you are right to be. You have been gone for a very long time, and I can only guess the terrible things they are imagining because that is the way parents are. But I have an idea."

Tobias was in such a state getting all the wedding presents packed up and loaded into carts and strapped to the backs of camels, together with the half of his fortune that Raguel had given them with the promise of the second half later on, that he found it hard to pay attention to what his father-in-law was saying. But when he heard how Raguel's voice faltered as he spoke and saw the slight trembling of his hands, he knew that it was something of great importance at least to Raguel and made a special effort to put his mind to it.

"How would it be if I sent a messenger to your father in Nineveh?" Raguel asked. "I have a very trustworthy man in mind, and he will be able to tell them everything that has been going on here in Ecbatana and can assure them that you are alive and well. Then, with your mind set at rest, you could stay on for a while longer. After all, there is no need to hurry."

Sarah was calling to Tobias from the house, and the dog, as he occasionally did, had taken his master's hand in his mouth, being careful not to hurt it with his teeth, as if to start leading him home then and there. For the first time it occurred to Tobias that Raguel would probably miss his daughter as much as Tobit and Anna had been missing him, but in his mind he had left Ecbatana already and couldn't even think of changing things now.

"I'm sorry, but I can't do that," he said. "I really just can't." And so it was that before the sun had reached its zenith, he and Sarah found themselves finally standing at the front door with Raguel and Edna and the servants and a number of neighbors all gathered in the street to make their farewells.

When Raguel had given him half of his fortune, it was by no means just money that was involved. There were oxen and sheep and goats as well as the black pony he had bought for Sarah as a child, which had grown fat and lost part of an ear over the years. There were also about a dozen of the slaves who tilled Raguel's fields or worked in his vineyards, and of course all the presents too and the boxes of Sarah's clothes that her father had helped her pack. All in all there was a train of baggage and beasts and people that would have impressed even Gabael.

Raguel had decided to make the best of it and with heroic effort managed to look almost cheerful. He took Sarah by both hands as she was about to climb into one of the carts and after kissing her on the brow said, "Be sure to honor your father-in-law and your mother-in-law, my beloved. They are your parents now." He could go no further.

Edna was delighted that after so many mishaps her daughter was finally a married woman, and in many ways she was delighted too to get her out of the house so that she would have Raguel all to herself again after so many years. But it was not without an ache in her heart that she too kissed Sarah good-bye and for once could find no words to add to her husband's but simply patted the young woman's cheek in an awkward way.

Her last words were to Tobias, who had already mounted one of the camels so that he would be too high off the ground for anyone to kiss, sitting astride there with one hand on the pommel and the blue scarf knotted at his throat.

"Travel safely," she said. "Make sure you bring your children back for us to see. May the good angels watch over you both."

She added then, "If there *are* good angels," which was the closest she had ever come in public to acknowledging her doubts on such matters.

"I am placing my only child in your hands," she continued, and would have continued still further about the various things he must be sure to do to ensure her comfort if Raguel had not caught her eye and put his finger to his lips. So she said only, "Don't ever do to anything to hurt her."

"I would sooner be eaten by a fish," Tobias said, and knocking his heels against the mangy ribs of his camel, he was off at last with the rest of the caravan behind him and the dog trotting along at his side.

ELEVEN

The Gall

A TRAIN OF BEASTS AND SLAVES AND CREAKING CARTS TOP-
heavy with baggage does not travel with the speed of two men
and a dog, and we went much more slowly on our homeward
way than we had in the other direction. Carts had to be prized
out of the mud, the cattle had to be watered, stray camels had
to be caught and herded back into line. There were times
when Sarah said that if she had to rattle along in the cart so
much as one more mile it would rattle the teeth right out of
her head, so, refusing to ride a camel like Tobias because she
claimed it made her seasick, she would get out and walk for a
while, and a slender young woman in sandals does not make
good time even with a husband at her side to carry her over

the rougher places. When many days had gone by and we were a good many still from Nineveh, I made a suggestion to Tobias. Why shouldn't he and I ride on ahead and get there maybe as much as a week sooner, leaving the others to follow at their own pace?

"The slaves are devoted to Sarah and will take the best of care of her," I said, and it was true. Raguel had never had them branded and their heads shaved bare and their ears pierced with an awl like others of their kind but had always treated them decently. There was also no danger of their running away because they had been slaves all their lives like their parents before them, and the idea of freedom terrified them.

"In addition to that," I said, "the sooner we get there, the better it will be for your parents, who by now must have given up all hope. It will also give them time to prepare their house to receive their new daughter-in-law. We will travel fast because we will take next to nothing with us. Except for one thing," I added, raising my forefinger in a schoolteacherly way because it seemed in keeping with Azarias's character.

Out of my saddle bag I drew a small sack tied at the neck and dangled it before Tobias. "Do you remember this?" I asked, and he replied that the smell was familiar.

"The liver and heart served us well as you will doubtless remember," I said. "This is the gall. I want you to take it from me now, and in good time I will tell you what to do with it."

Tobias took it with a grimace and then trotted back on his camel to the cart where Sarah was gripping on to both sides for dear life and explained to her what I had proposed. At first she didn't like the idea at all. It would be the first time she had been separated from her husband since their wedding, and from the way she clung to him you would have thought he was leaving forever, and from the way he took her in his arms you would have thought he thought so too.

But gradually the idea of being able to travel at a less exhausting pace began to appeal to her, and so did the idea of giving Tobias's parents a little advance warning before they were descended upon not only by a new daughter-in-law but by the whole menagerie she had with her. It would also give her some time herself to collect her wits and think about what she would say and what she would wear and how she might conduct herself in a way to make the best possible impression when they met for the first time. So it was finally agreed upon between them, and after many lingering farewells, Tobias and I rode off on our camels and he told the dog to stay behind and lend Sarah his support.

It happened that on the day the two of us arrived in Nineveh, Tobit had gone with his wife to keep vigil at the northern gate, not that his blind eyes could be of any use to her in spotting us on the road if we came into view but simply to keep her company. The first thing Anna saw was a cloud of dust way off in the distance, but since she had seen such clouds many times before, she didn't dare get her hopes up or even mention it to Tobit. After a while, when she saw, or thought she saw, that there were two figures in the cloud, though still far away, her heart gave a little leap, but when she could make out that they were mounted, it sank again, and she told Tobit yet one more time that the situation was hopeless.

It was when she could make out that one of the two seemed to be wearing something blue that she clutched Tobit's arm so tightly that it made him wince because she remembered about the blue scarf and the forward young woman who had given it. But it was plain to see that there was no dog at their side, and she could not believe that her son would dream of returning without him.

It was a beggar who claimed to be blind who first recognized them for sure. In spite of the head cloth she pulled over her face for disguise, he had long since known that it was Anna who came there day after day, and he also knew perfectly well what she was waiting for because the Jews of Nineveh always kept careful track of each other's comings and goings, and Tobias's trip was no secret and neither was his long overdue return. When the beggar heard the little gasp she gave out as she clutched her husband's arm, he pushed back up on his forehead the rag that he normally kept tied over his eyes for professional reasons, and after taking a hard look said, "As I live and breathe, there he is at last and as fine a camel under him as any I've seen for years."

How to describe the effect of this upon Anna? She didn't even take time to tell Tobit, who knew well enough anyway as soon as she let go of his arm and with a single cry went running off with such speed that her head cloth was blown to the ground and her uncombed hair flew out in the air behind her. How to describe the look on Tobias's face when he saw her coming or the look on hers when she almost pulled him down off the camel and covered his face with her tears as she all but squeezed the breath out of him hugging him with both arms? I stayed a little way off as they raced back to Tobit, who was staggering around with his hands stretched before him to keep from running into the wall or one of the immoral women. There are times when even the angels think it best to avert their eyes.

It wasn't until we got back to the house that I started playing the part of Azarias again, nor would it have made any difference if I had done so earlier because none of the three of them had shown the slightest awareness of my presence. While Anna was at the oven burning dinner in her frenzy and Tobit was knocking things over in his search for the best wine, I asked Tobias to step out into the courtyard for a moment.

"That gall that I gave you," I said, pointing to the bulge under his shirt where I knew he kept it. "When the moment seems right, I want you to take some of it on each of your thumbs and rub it into your father's eyes." When Tobias looked at me with utter disbelief, I asked, "Have I ever failed you?" And when he could only shake his head slowly from side to side for an answer, I added, "Then just do as I say, and we will see what we will see."

The moment that seemed right to him came when we had just sat down to our meal. Tobias had not gotten around yet to telling them much at all about his adventures, and they were waiting in silence for him to begin when he rose from his seat and went around behind his father. I could see in his face that he was trying to decide whether to explain to him what he was on the point of doing or just to go ahead and do it. I suppose he thought that any explanation would make Tobit think that the long journey had driven him mad, so without a word he simply dipped both his thumbs into the malodorous contents of the bag and before anyone could guess what he was up to smeared it generously into both Tobit's eyes.

Tobit screamed as though he had been stabbed. He leapt up from the table, knocking over his chair, and stumbled about the kitchen grinding both of his fists into his sockets with such force that I was afraid he might do himself permanent damage. When Anna rushed up with a pitcher of water for flushing them out, he thrust her aside and went on grinding his fists and shouting in pain until finally in exhaustion he let his hands drop to his sides and stood there staring at us. The white films on his eyes were like the white underskins of an onion, and even as we watched, they began to fall away, beginning at the corners, as if some invisible hand was peeling them off. Once more he dug his fists into his sockets and then, when he stopped, shouted out not in pain but in stupefaction. He could hardly get the words out of his mouth, but they were addressed to the Holy One when they came.

"You afflicted me because my unworthiness deserved affliction," he said in a voice thick with emotion, "and now you have restored my sight because your nature is always to be merciful to those who please you."

He was totally wrong on both counts, of course. The Holy One does not go around afflicting people, and although his nature is indeed above all else merciful, Tobit was a good man and in no more need of mercy than a two-year-old child. What he needed was simply someone who understood the therapeutic powers of fish gall.

So great was their rejoicing at this cure, which they believed to be as miraculous as in truth it was just a matter of having somebody there who knew what he was doing, that it was some time before they remembered to ask Tobias what he had been up to all the weeks he was away and whether he had brought back the two sacks of silver from Gabael and all the rest of it. Before they reached that point, however, their constant ejaculations of praise addressed to the Holy One were touching in their way but only went to show once again that by and large the world believes in him for all the wrong reasons and that, like Raguel and Edna, it disbelieves in him for all the wrong reasons too.

It was not until we had finished our burnt dinner that Tobias finally got the chance to tell his story. He began by saying that the sacks of silver would be arriving almost any time and that they were by no means all that would be arriving. The fish, the side trip to Rages, the icy streams and crowded bazaars, the maidservant who looked like a wrestler, the munificence of Gabael not to mention his upholstered wagon and the six horses that pulled it with its canopy on top and side curtains—Tobias had never made such a long speech in his life, and to keep his throat from going dry, he drank rather a good deal more of his father's wine than he was accustomed to and interrupted himself from time to time with inappropriate laughter and gestures entirely out of keeping with his character.

He saved the most extraordinary thing he had to tell them for last. In Ecbatana, he said, we had stayed with a distant cousin of Tobit's named Raguel, and at the sound of that name Tobit's newly recovered eyes lit up because he remembered about Raguel and remembered too something about a daughter of his who was said to have had marital problems. Her name was Sarah, Tobias told him, and then went into the whole matter of the seven husbands and the demon Asmodeus, who had the teeth of a lion and a scorpion's tail. He ended with Sarah herself.

"We got married," he said with a little more of the inappropriate laughter. "There was a party that lasted for fourteen full days and most of the nights too, and if you want to know the truth, she is on her way here right this minute with a lot of carts and animals and more junk than you could shake a stick at. In fact she will probably be arriving before the week is out."

It was almost too much in one day for Tobit and Anna, and when Tobias went on to tell them how Raguel had already given him half of his fortune, they both had to go to their bed and lie down though not before asking for endless details about the bride and her parents and the two weeks of feasting. From time to time they also slipped in some discreet questions as to just what half of Raguel's fortune actually came to and in what form it had come.

Tobit's estimate of his bride's arrival turned out to be overly optimistic. Sarah did not arrive by the end of the week nor by the end of the next week either, so slow was their progress what with one thing or another including a kicking fight between two of the slaves over the wife of one of them that ended up with so many injuries for both men that it was necessary to pause for the better part of a week so they could recover. It was not until the start of the third week that the caravan finally came into view, and again it was the blind beggar who broke the news, having spotted it from his usual place at the northern gate while it was still some distance away and having run all the way to their house to tell them. Tobit and Anna, followed by Tobias and me, reached the two winged bulls just in time to see the procession starting to make its cumbersome way through the passage between them.

Needless to say, Sarah had dressed for the occasion with exceptional care. She had spent so long brushing her hair that it was as if there was starlight in it, and the gown she wore was one that her father had given her. It was a far paler blue than her husband's scarf and had long, fringed sleeves and a deep hem sewn with pink shells, and around her throat hung Gabael's emerald like a burst of green fire.

Tobit found that everything he had set eyes on since the gall had done its work gave him unimaginable pleasure, even the dust on the cupboard shelf, or the rusty latch of the out-house door, or his own bare feet, even the droppings of the sparrows. But when he first saw his son's wife being handed down out of her cart by one of the slaves, it seemed to him as if for the first time in his entire experience the invisible musicians were playing with such incomparable skill that he made a series of frantic, beckoning gestures to tell them to keep coming, keep doing it right, keep sounding like the angels who sing at the throne of Glory, as indeed we do. Sarah thought he must be having a fit until his words reassured her.

"Blessed be the Holy One who has brought you to us," he said, "and blessed are your father and mother." This particularly touched her because she had thought many times about her father along the way and more than a few times about her mother. Then he went straight to where she stood and kissed her first on her brow and then on each of her hands, which astounded all the beggars, peddlers, ambiguous women, and gossiping old men who up to that point had believed he was still blind.

As far as Tobias was concerned, the only thing that in any way marred an occasion that otherwise gave him as much pleasure as anything that had happened since he and Sarah first made their way into each other's arms was his parents' decision to celebrate with a feast. Because their means were as modest as Raguel's were impressive, they thought they couldn't possibly afford fourteen days, much to Tobias's relief, but they felt they could manage at least seven now if Tobit decided to go back to being a purchasing agent for the king and if Anna kept turning out shawls for the court ladies. They neither of them altogether believed yet in the reality of the two sacks of silver.

So while the baggage and presents were being stored away wherever room could be made for them, and while pasturage was found for the new cattle and quarters for the slaves, and while the silver was being carefully counted and eventually buried by Tobit with the same shovel that he had so often used for the graves—while all this, as I say, was in progress, so was the feasting.

There was such an abundance of food and drink that once again Tobit went back to his old routine of distributing the overflow to the poor. He could only hope that the Holy One had forgotten all about the prayer that he had prayed to die when Anna had insulted him over the goat, and that he would be permitted to go on doing good deeds indefinitely. He prayed now that he be granted years enough to play with the grandchildren whom at last he dared hope he might live to see, and to show them off to his friends.

Among the many friends he entertained during the seven days was his influential nephew Ahikar, who was second only to the king in power. Ahikar had recently had his left hand cut off at the wrist for some breach of court etiquette, but even so he retained the complete confidence of Esarhaddon, who laughingly referred to him as his right-hand man. In spite of this new handicap and a rank so exalted that he preferred never to be caught doing anything so plebeian as enjoying himself, Ahikar was clearly having the time of his life.

He threw back his head covered with matted hair and laughed like a bass drum being struck by a shoe when Tobias showed him how he had taught the dog to sit up. He whispered in Tobias's ear that the dog did it more impressively than the king on his throne and then asked that his cup be refilled to the brim.

TWELVE

Azarias Unmasked

Thanks to Raguel's generosity, Tobias found that he had more money than he knew what to do with, but he knew what to do with some of it.

Since his parents' modest house was clearly not large enough to accommodate Sarah and himself in addition to all the presents, clothes, bedding, and assorted chattels that they had brought with them from Ecbatana, he decided to look for a new house that would not only have the space they needed for themselves but also quarters for the slaves. As Sarah pointed out, it was foolish to go on paying good money to board them elsewhere. They also hoped that they could find a house that came with land enough for grazing the cattle.

What they did first was look at a number of places in Nineveh itself although not all parts of the city were open to them because, as Jews, they were members of a captive people, and the Assyrians tended to regard them with a combination of fear, condescension, and guilt, not to mention a certain degree of envy stemming from their unusually sharp wits and superior resourcefulness, qualities they had been obliged to develop in order to survive captivity.

They found a large establishment down near the king's vast stables that for a time they thought might be just what they were after. It had more than enough rooms for their own use and also for their children if they proved fortunate enough to have any. Moreover, it contained a number of considerably smaller rooms out in back that would be perfectly adequate for the slaves and any servants they might later acquire. Adjacent to the paddocks, where the king's horses spent their days munching at the grass and swishing at the flies with their flowing tails, there was also a broad tract of land just right for the cattle.

Unfortunately, however, the house itself was built near the river, and on the second or third time they went down to look it over and plan which rooms might be used for what purpose and so on, several water rats went scrambling across the floor with such malevolent expressions on their faces that Sarah fled to her husband's arms in terror, and the dog, after making a rather unconvincing show of pursuing them, took refuge in the courtyard outside, which gave him an unobstructed view in all directions of anything that might be heading his way. So that was the end of that, and all the other places that for a time they considered turned out for one reason or another to be equally unacceptable.

It was Anna who suggested that they try looking outside the city. Once she and Tobit had time to digest the fact that the buried silver was indeed, as Tobit had always maintained, far more than enough to support all of them in comfort for the rest of their lives, she decided that she could afford to give up her work for the court ladies except for an occasional shawl which she ran up on her loom as a special favor, and she had so much time on her hands that she took to scouting about on her own to see if she could find anything that would meet the young pair's requirements. After several false leads, she finally found it.

It was a big, sprawling place no more than a mile or two from the northern gate with a pleasing view of the city and the river that wound its slow, silver way beyond it, and what won Sarah's heart the very first time she saw it was that it was built on a hillside that reminded her of the one that Raguel used to take her to as a child when she would paddle around in the pond in her drawers and chase moths. On his part, Tobias noted that even if their flocks were to double in number, there was plenty of pasturage to sustain them. So, getting Ahikar's help in negotiating a price with the owner, who was eager to endear himself to a man of such influence with the king, they bought it at a great bargain and in due course moved in with all their possessions.

It may be wondered what I was doing all this time in my role as Azarias, and the answer is that I was not doing much of anything for the reason that my mission had been so nearly accomplished that there wasn't much left for me except to wait for the right moment to do one last thing. It may be wondered too how it was that the prayers of the world continued to reach the Holy One all the months that I was occupied elsewhere, and the answer to that is twofold. In the first place, there were the six other archangels to take on the work in my absence including Gabriel, who announces to the world when something of surpassing wonder is about to happen, and Michael, who with his sword of flame is in constant battle with the powers of darkness, of whom none other than Asmodeus, of course, is the acknowledged lord. In the second place, it is my conviction that even if all seven of us were unavailable for some reason, the prayers would reach the Holy One anyway because there is no cry from the human heart that he does not hear even if the humans involved happen to be unbelievers like Raguel and Edna and wouldn't be caught dead praying in any way that either they or anyone else would recognize as such. But back to the one final thing that remained for me to do and how I waited until the right moment came for doing it.

Tobias and Sarah had of course given me a room in their house because they were both of them hospitable by nature and also felt greatly beholden to me. From time to time, I suspect, they secretly looked forward to the day when I would finally move on to something else so that they could enjoy each other's company all by themselves, but in the meanwhile they couldn't have treated me more cordially despite the rather officious manner that I continued to affect as Azarias and the habit I perfected of raising my forefinger at them whenever their attention wandered. Tobias encouraged me to go fishing with him in the Tigris and enlisted my help in supervising the work of the slaves in his fields and vineyards even though he was entirely capable, in his easygoing way, of doing it perfectly well by himself. When Sarah found that she was with child, she made a point of constantly asking my advice about the care and feeding of infants as though we weren't both aware that no one was better qualified to instruct her in such matters than Anna.

The moment I had been waiting for came one late afternoon when the three of us were sitting on the terrace that looked out toward the city with nothing in particular to do except watch the dog race around and around the house with breathtaking speed because he had nothing particular to do either. Earlier that day, Tobias had gone to see his father for advice on what wages he thought he should offer the maidservant they were thinking of hiring to help Sarah around the house because she was troubled by morning sickness and found it difficult to do all the work by herself. Tobit told him what he thought would be fair and then suddenly brought up my name.

"Speaking of wages," he said. "I have been thinking about the drachma a day plus expenses that I paid Azarias. It seemed like a reasonable amount at the time, but considering all that he has done for all of us and the time he has had to spend doing it, I think we have grossly shortchanged him."

As Tobias turned the matter over in his mind, twisting a bit of his springy hair around and around one finger, he realized that even before his father had brought it up, he had had uneasy feelings about me along the same lines. Then one by one he ticked off on his fingers all the services I had rendered.

"He got me safely to Ecbatana and back," he said. "He saved me from being gobbled down by the fish. He got Gabael to give me the money with absolutely no fuss at all. He found me a wife and took care of that demon whose name I can never get straight. And he showed me the way to get rid of the white films on your eyes with those putrid guts."

Looking dazed for a moment or two as he relived these various adventures, he suddenly slapped both hands down on his knees. He said, "What I'm going to do is give him half of everything Raguel gave me, not a penny less. And still we'll be getting off cheap."

Helpful as I had been, the amount seemed a little excessive to Tobit, but remembering all that Tobias would still have left and how terrible it had been to be blind, and thinking too of the two sacks of silver he had scarcely yet touched, he approved his son's decision and said so. It was the afternoon of that same day that Tobias made the offer to me.

I could not think of turning it down, of course, because that would have robbed him of the chance of showing me his gratitude the way he wanted to, but, on the other hand, what possible use does an angel have for money? So I decided that the moment had come to do what I had had in mind for a long time. I was sitting between Tobias and Sarah on a bench and took each of their hands in one of mine.

"I guess I had better make a clean breast of it," I said. "I've been living under false pretenses long enough."

Sarah placed her free hand on her stomach where she thought she could feel the baby stirring. Tobias gave me a puzzled frown.

"It is good to know that you recognize all that has been done for you," I said, "and this offer you've made is generous to a fault, but I'm afraid you're making it to the wrong party. There at the fishmonger's stall many months ago, it wasn't Azarias who came to your rescue but somebody else. Or maybe I should say that the person you know as Azarias was at the fishmonger's stall only because somebody else had sent him."

"What on earth are you talking about?" Tobias asked.

"I am talking about the Holy One, blessed be he," I said. "He was the one who sent me, and he is the one you should be thanking now."

Tobias had never given much time to religious speculation any more than he had ever found prayers anything but a kind of tedious obligation that his father seemed to think important, and it was clear that he was more confused than interested by what I had said.

"There would be no point in my giving the Holy One half of my half of Raguel's fortune, I suppose," he said. "He must have everything he could possibly want already."

"There is little question about that," I said. "But if you were to give it to somebody else instead, the chances are he would be just as pleased if not more so."

"Have you any suggestions?" Tobias inquired. The dog had just come racing around the house for something like the fiftieth time, his long tongue flapping hilariously.

"Your father could help you with that," I said. "Just watch where he goes with those armfuls of secondhand clothes and leftovers from the table. Even the king can be generous once in a while because almost nobody's heart is entirely black. Besides, he thinks it might keep him on the good side of those stone bulls of his or whatever absurd statuary he is worshiping these days. So you might also ask your father's nephew Ahikar for suggestions. He will tell you about the people that Esarhaddon sends him to now and then with money to hand out—the old men who can't work anymore and the women who sell themselves at the gate for money to feed their babies."

"There are plenty of them around," Tobias said. "I have always tried to choose the streets where I won't be likely to see them."

"Try other streets," I said.

"It would be awful," Sarah said, "to have nothing to feed your baby."

"At least I've given you something to think about," I said, and for a while they sat there in silence while they were thinking. Tired of running at last, the dog flopped down at his master's feet and lay there panting.

"Here's one more thing while you're at it," I said. "Ahikar would tell you how important it is to guard the secrets of a king like treasure because if ever you give them away, you'll end up with your head on the end of a sharpened stick or at least minus a hand or two. But with the Holy One it's another kettle of fish entirely."

"Exactly what do you mean?" Tobias asked. The sun had begun to sink lower over Nineveh, and the silver river was changing to something more like bronze.

"I mean that though you must never tell the secrets of a king," I said, "nothing is more pleasing to the Holy One than when you tell about the secret things he is always doing for people or trying to do if they give him half a chance. I am thinking about all the things he has done for you and your family, for instance. Tell people about those things and never forget them yourself. Tell them how even on the darkest stretches of the road to Ecbatana, he was always at your side if you'd only had the eyes to see him." I started to raise my finger at them to be sure I got the point across, but then I remembered that I no longer had to be Azarias and had spoken like a schoolteacher enough already.

"I suppose I understand you more or less in some sort of way," Tobias said, "but there's one thing I still don't get at all, and here it is. If you weren't really Azarias there in the market the first time I saw you—isn't that what you said?—then who in the world are you?"

The right moment had come at last, and letting go of their hands, I got up off the bench to answer them. I spoke first to Sarah.

"When you went out into the sheep shed and thought about hanging yourself because those disagreeable maidservants had accused you, and not entirely without justice, of murdering your seven first husbands," I said, "I was as close to you as the rope you'd thrown over the beam, but you didn't see me."

I could tell she was struggling to remember how it had been back then and how, after deciding that to hang herself would be to break her father's heart, she had prayed to die young instead.

"I was also with Tobit every time he sneaked off in the night to bury the dead and again when he prayed in the outhouse to die himself, like Sarah, because Anna had insulted him. And you too, Tobias," I went on. "Even before you could walk I was always hovering around you somewhere though you never seemed to need me as much as most others."

"You still haven't told me who you are though," Tobias said, and he and his wife sat side by side on the bench watching me with their puzzled young eyes as they waited for me to tell them.

"I am Raphael," I said. "I am one of the seven archangels. My task is to carry to the throne of glory the prayers of all people who pray and also of those who don't even know that they're praying."

When I could tell that either they didn't quite believe me or didn't quite want to believe me or thought that perhaps my wits had begun to turn or that their wits were turning, I decided the time had come to let them see who I was with their own eyes.

What they saw of me was about as much as a child's hand can hold of the sea, but it was enough. A fire burned before them like no other fire. A fragrance fresher than the roses of Sharon filled the air, and the leaves of the trees tossed like plumes though there was no wind stirring. There was the sound of as many voices singing as there are stars in the sky. There was a silence deeper than the deepest well.

Their wonder was so great that they both hid their faces in their hands. Even the dog placed his paws over his eyes.

"Don't be afraid," I told them, and when finally they took their hands from their faces, I was gone.

THIRTEEN

Tobit Rambles On

Sᴏᴍᴇ ᴘʀᴀʏᴇʀs ᴀʀᴇ sᴏ ɪɴᴛᴇʀᴍɪɴᴀʙʟᴇ ᴛʜᴀᴛ I ᴄᴀʀʀʏ ᴛʜᴇᴍ ᴀ little at a time, not certainly to save my own strength, which is in no need of saving, but out of consideration for the Holy One, who undoubtedly considers my thoughtfulness wrong-headed. "Why shouldn't people pray for as long as they want?" he might well say if he spoke in words instead of in silences that are like the rushing of wind through a forest. Why shouldn't they indeed?

A year or so after I disappeared forever as Azarias, Tobit got to going over in his mind everything that had happened, both the bad things like getting sparrow droppings in his eyes and the good things like having lived to see Tobias's first child, who was a boy. He thought of cruel people like Esarhaddon, who had mutilated Ahikar for some trifle, and of dishonest people like the blind beggar who could see farther than a hawk. He thought of vain people like the court ladies, who were always after Anna to make them a new shawl though they knew she had virtually gone out of business or trying to persuade her to dye an old one a more fashionable color. He thought about warmhearted people like his own wife, who had worked so hard to keep their bodies and souls together when he was unable to work at all, and like Raguel, whom he had never set eyes on but who had been so openhanded with Tobias, and about the poor people by the river who rarely complained of their lot and yet seemed more at peace in their unwashed skins than most of the rich in their palaces and would give you the shirts off their backs if only they had shirts to give. He thought about his entire people, the Jews, who had been carried off from Samaria to a godless land where every hand was raised against them, and about their kindred to the south, who would probably be swallowed up next. He thought about the temple they were so proud of and how it would almost certainly be left a smoldering ruin before many more years had passed. Most of all, of course, he thought about the Holy One, who he believed watches every move people make like the most vigilant overseer of slaves and is perpetually keeping track of their every misstep.

All of these matters and more he put into a single prayer that he prayed one night when Anna was sleeping in their bed and no one in all Nineveh seemed to be stirring except for himself. He echoed the stately cadences that he had heard from the priests long ago in Jerusalem and used a great many of their words which at the time he had memorized just as he had also made many of their religious notions his own. I would not dream of setting down the whole unwieldy utterance, but a snippet or two will perhaps suffice to suggest the heart-wrenching absurdity of most of it.

To start with, instead of calling the Holy One by one of his many names and speaking to him like the friend one would have hoped he knew him now to be, Tobit spoke to him in the third person for fear that he might think him too familiar otherwise. A man can't be too careful, he believed.

"Blessed be God" was how he began, and he looked up at the sky wondering for a moment if there was anyone there to hear him. He believed that there was and would have wagered as much as his grandson's life that there was if such an unthinkable wager had been forced upon him, and yet the darkness over his head seemed so vast and indifferent that something inside him faltered as he spoke, and he could only hope that it wouldn't be set down on the record against him. Nor was he entirely sure what it meant to call the Holy One blessed or whether it made any sense to tell him something about himself that he must already know.

"For he afflicts and shows mercy," he went on, "and there is no one who can escape his hand."

What he saw in his mind was the way he himself sometimes went about in the kitchen swatting flies with a shoe,
afflicting them in the sense of squashing them flat because he
found their presence irritating. Plenty of them escaped his
hand, needless to say, because he was only a man and his aim
far from perfect, but in addition to the ones who escaped that
way there would also from time to time be some particular fly
dozing in the sun or rubbing its feet together oblivious of anything else, and it would look so meager and pitiable and
unsuspecting that Tobit would withhold his shoe and pass on.
He liked to believe that the Holy One might decide to spare
him for somewhat the same reason. As to the others, if the
Holy One found them irritating, why shouldn't he squash
them flat? For that matter if he found an entire people irritating, why shouldn't he do the same thing to the whole lot of
them? And that was what Tobit turned to next, addressing
himself not to the Holy One any longer but to his own people.

"Acknowledge him before the nations, O sons of Israel,
for he has scattered us among them," he said. In other words,
he believed that it was the Holy One himself who had made
the decision that they were to be scattered, and that was how
it came about that the Assyrians had dragged them away from
their comfortable homes and fertile fields and trundled them
off to Nineveh, where they were reduced to living under the
most marginal conditions along the banks of the Tigris. As
Tobit gave it some thought, it appeared that in this matter the
Holy One sounded less like a man swatting flies than like a

man trapping water rats in his stable and carrying them off in a cage to deal with when he got around to it.

"He will afflict us for our iniquities," he went on.

He was sitting on the overturned rain barrel and as far away from the vine-covered wall as possible because of the sparrows. Iniquities were of course at the heart of it, he understood. His people had angered the Holy One by behaving in an iniquitous way. There were men among them who carried on with women who were not their wives and often not much more than half their age. There were others who neglected to pray for days at a time, sometimes for weeks, because they had other things on their minds perhaps or were too busy earning a living or weren't sure what the Holy One expected them to say. There were women who seemed to be born ill-tempered and others who were so preoccupied with their complexions and their clothes and their social standing that they gave no thought whatever to anything else, least of all to the unfortunate souls who turned up at their back doors when the cook was throwing out scraps for the dogs. It was no wonder the Holy One had scattered his people, Tobit thought. He had simply had all he could take.

He could hear the faint mutter of Anna's snoring from inside the house. She had gone back to doing things with her hair again and slept with only one unyielding pillow at the nape of her neck in order to disarrange it as little as possible. She was not perfect by a long shot, Tobit thought—who was for that matter?—but surely there must be something about the way she looked when she was tired or the way she hummed under her breath when she was at her loom that would turn aside the Holy One's anger. There must be something about himself also, he hoped, and about Tobias, and certainly at the very least about Tobias's son, who was still so young that it was hard to believe that he had had time yet to anger anybody.

"If you turn to him with all your heart, to do what is true before him, then he will turn to you and will not hide his face from you," Tobit said, recalling verbatim one of the prayers he had heard in the temple long before. He was thinking about his grandson again, who had his mother's dark eyes and something of his father too in the easygoing way he crawled around the garden as if he didn't have a care in the world, which as far as Tobit knew he didn't.

If only the child would turn to the Holy One when he grew up and had good sense. If only he would do just two or three things a day right when the Scorekeeper's eye was upon him. If only the Holy One would find some one small thing about him comparable to the fly's rubbing its legs together that would soften his heart. Then he, the Holy One, might turn, in reward, to his grandson and not hide his face from him the way he seemed to have hidden it from Tobit himself during the years when he was stumbling blindly around the kitchen knocking over furniture or stepping on the dog's tail.

But that terrible *if* jarred his ears as he spoke it like one of the invisible flute players blowing a flat where there was supposed to be a sharp, and Tobit made a sour face in the dark where no one could see it. Who could tell to what the child might turn or to whom when the time came around? *If* was the hinge that the fate of the whole world hung on. If it behaved itself, the doors of Heaven would swing open. If it failed to in even the slightest degree, they would be slammed shut in its face.

But the Holy One was supposed to be beyond all else merciful, Tobit remembered, and he tried to concentrate on that as he rose from the barrel to relieve himself under the mulberry tree. When he returned, he addressed himself once more to his people and thought about them in their beds with the innocence of sleep on their faces, dreaming their dreams. He felt he must say something in his prayer that would raise their spirits if they could only hear him. He felt he must say something that would raise his own spirits.

"May he cheer those within you who are captives," he said, "and love those within you who are distressed, to all generations forever." Then he repeated the words "Love those within you who are distressed" a second time because of all the words he had spoken thus far, they were the ones that he found most comforting. Maybe the tide would turn, he allowed himself to dream. Maybe at least for his grandson's generation things would go better, starting out with a clean record as they were, and for a moment or two he reassured himself with wild and hopeful conjectures. Maybe they would live to see a day when the Holy One decided to love them for what they were instead of to afflict them for what they were not. Who could guess what glorious things he might do for them once he got started in a new direction?

"Many nations will come from afar to the name of the Lord God," he heard himself saying. He shifted his weight slightly on the barrel to ease his buttocks and then added, "Bearing gifts in their hands, gifts for the King of Heaven," which was one of the Holy One's many names.

Maybe the time would come, Tobit mused, when all nations would recognize that in spite of its many faults, for which it was continually apologizing, his nation possessed something or was possessed by something that was worth coming from afar to find even if it meant coming on your knees across the fiery sands of the desert. And that something was the Holy One himself. Maybe even the Assyrians, not to mention the Medes and the Babylonians and the Egyptians and all the rest of them, would eventually see that their gods had no more to offer than had the stone bulls that guarded the northern gate. Then they too would raise their voices in praise of the Holy One at last, bringing him gifts as precious as Gabael's emerald. The captivity of his people would come to an end at last, and their onetime captors, maybe even Esarhaddon himself, would stand at the gate waving good-bye as they set out on their long journey back to the comfortable homes they had left years before where they would sweep out the mouse droppings and mend the long-neglected roofs and replant their gardens.

It was the invisible harps that were playing now, and Tobit let his eyes fall shut as he listened to the muted plucking of the strings, waving one hand dreamily back and forth through the air to keep time.

As long as he was at it, he thought, he might as well let his imagination run wild. He thought about the city of Jerusalem the way he had known it as a young man when he traveled south from Samaria with unblemished lambs to sacrifice at the temple and a tenth part of all his grain and vegetables. Jerusalem was the city of King David, soon after whose death everything had more or less fallen to pieces with the nation dividing into one kingdom in the south and another in the north, and nothing was ever the same again. The city was the life-giving heart of his people, and Tobit could hardly think of it without tears coming to his eyes even as they came to them now, trickling down his cheeks where he wiped them away with his sleeve. He remembered the clamorous streets, and the steep hills, and the priests in their elaborate hats, and the palace of the king with walls that they said could never be toppled. More than anything else, he remembered the temple that Solomon had built with its tall golden doors and floors of cypress and the huge olivewood angels guarding a small room so holy that only the high priest was allowed to enter it and then only once in the entire year and for only a very short time. He remembered the bronze sea in the court, which stood for the waters of chaos whose power the Holy One had to harness before he could make the world. He could almost smell the flowers and incense on the altar and hear the singing of the aproned priests with their long beards.

Given the unrelenting rapacity and general nastiness of men, Tobit thought, and given also the limited patience of the Holy One, the time was bound to come when Jerusalem would fall like Samaria before it and jackals would prowl in its ruins. But so sweet was the sound of the harps, joined now by the horns as soft as a woman humming—he welcomed the horns with a single raised finger—that he could not bring himself to dwell on such sad matters and went on with his dreaming instead.

"Jerusalem will be built with sapphires and emeralds and her towers and battlements with pure gold," he said. He meant a second Jerusalem, even fairer than the first, which the Holy One himself would cause to be built out of pity for his favorite if most troublesome people, believing that at last they had been afflicted long enough for their sins.

"The streets will be paved with beryl and ruby and the stone of Ophir," he said, tapping the rain barrel lightly with one hand to the rhythm of these beautiful words. He wasn't sure what the stone of Ophir was, but he knew it must be something of surpassing splendor. "All her lanes will cry 'Hallelujah!' in praise of the One who has exalted her forever."

Then he said the word "forever" once again because it seemed a particularly fitting one for bringing to an end this prayer, which in reality had gone on immeasurably longer than these few short extracts can convey.

His colorful picture of a new Jerusalem coming down out of the sky as fresh and lovely as Sarah coming down out of the cart in her blue dress when she first arrived at Nineveh as a bride was as close as he got to the actual truth of things. Gone, at least for the moment, was his view of the Holy One as a man swatting flies or trapping rats in the stable or flying into a temper as savage as any Assyrian king's. Gone too was the notion of the Holy One keeping score so exactingly that not even the angels could escape the severest penalties.

In place of all this, at least for as long as it took him to go back into the house, he thought about how the Holy One, blessed be he, wishes the world and its creatures nothing but well. He thought also how, though never condoning the shadows that dwell in the human heart, he is forever dispatching angels of light to deal with them mercifully.

If that didn't work, Tobit thought as he slipped into bed beside Anna, who could tell but that maybe when the right time arrived, the Holy One might in some unimaginable way come down and deal with them mercifully himself?

With that extraordinary notion, which brought a faint, crooked smile to his lips, he laid his head down on the pillow and was soon sleeping as soundly as his wife.

FOURTEEN

A Few Last Words

Tobias and Sarah produced five sons before they were done, and although Tobias had no trouble remembering their names, having chosen them himself with his wife's help, there were times when it took him a moment or two to remember which name belonged to which. They were amiable, free-wheeling boys like their father, and Tobit lived long enough not only to see them all grown into manhood but even to have children of their own who were the chief delight of his old age.

He would take them walking along the banks of the river where they would poke at frogs with their toes for the pleasure of hearing them plunk back into the water. Sometimes he and

Anna would lead them down to the palace where some of the court ladies for whom Anna continued to make shawls as a special favor arranged to have them admitted to a balcony with an excellent view of the king passing by after some successful skirmish with the Medes. Leaning so far out over the railing that their great-grandparents had to grab them by their shirttails to keep them from falling, the goggle-eyed children would watch the king with his lamb's-wool beard leading a long procession of captives in chains, carts loaded with spoil, and even an occasional elephant, which was a special treat for the children, who marveled at the great piles of dung they left in their wake and the way their trunks swung back and forth with a life of their own.

Tobit gave up burying the dead in the dark of night both because at his age the digging didn't come as easily as it once had and also because, thanks to his nephew Ahikar's intercession on their behalf, there were many fewer Jews executed than in the old days, but he continued with his benefactions among the poor, and sometimes Tobias would go along to help carry the baskets.

Another delight of Tobit's later years was to see how Tobias continued to prosper. The flocks that Raguel had given him multiplied to such an extent that he was obliged to buy ever more land for grazing them, and his crops grew abundantly too. His vines produced grapes of such remarkable quality that they fetched a higher price in the market than the grapes of anyone else.

Tobit also took particular pleasure in the presence of Sarah. She became the daughter that he and Anna had never had, and he in turn filled part at least of the place in her heart where she still missed her father. Almost every year she would make the journey back to Ecbatana to see him and show off her children and later her grandchildren to him and Edna, but it was not the way it had been in the days when just the two of them would wander off to the willow grove and talk to each other about everything under the sun.

All in all these years were as happy as any that Tobit had ever known, and he could hardly remember the days of his blindness when they had been forced to scrimp by on Anna's modest earnings. Once in a while he thought back to the dismal time when he had shut himself up in the outhouse and prayed to the Holy One for death, and then he would thank his lucky stars that the Holy One had either not happened to hear him, or in his mercy had decided to ignore him, or possibly had forgotten all about it.

But even in the midst of his happiness, there were shadows. He continued to fear that someday, like one of the flies in his kitchen, he would do something so irritating to the Holy One that he would come after him with a shoe, and he regretted all the occasions when he had also irritated Anna to the point that she had menaced him with her wooden spoon. Despite all the good deeds he had done among the poor and continued to do, he thought about the innumerable good deeds he had never gotten around to doing and could only hope that when the Holy One added things up at the final count, his bad marks would not outweigh by too much the good ones. There was also the misadventure that befell Ahikar, which for a while cast a shadow over all the Jews in the city.

The story is too complicated to set down in detail, but the gist of it is this. Ahikar continued virtually to run the country for the king, who in turn continued to recognize that his services were indispensable, but Ahikar had a nephew named Nadab, who threatened for a while to destroy the whole happy arrangement. He was no blood kin of Tobit's, for which Tobit was grateful, and also a very unstable young man with hair as long as Asmodeus's and an equally chilling smile. Ahikar had never married partly because his work left him little time for such things and partly because the few women he had approached on the subject were put off by the way his hair lay flat on his head like a piece of old carpet. As a consequence he made his nephew Nadab his heir and did all he could to advance him in the court. Dreaming that perhaps he could replace his uncle in the king's favor, Nadab forged a number of letters addressed to the kings of Egypt and Persia full of highly classified information about the strengths and weaknesses and future plans of the Assyrian army and saw to it that they fell into the king's hands. The signature that he set down at the end was of course Ahikar's. Never one to waste time when even the faintest suspicion of treason was involved, the king immediately had Ahikar thrown into jail to await the peculiarly hideous death that he had in mind for him. There are various fanciful versions of how the unfortunate man managed it, but by one means or another he escaped into hiding, and for long months there was no one to speak words of moderation and sanity into the king's ear, least of all Nadab, who was himself so far from sane that even the king noticed it and banished him from court with both of his ears missing.

That was the only sensible move the king made, however. Because of the treasonous letters, he saw an enemy behind every tree, and no one came under darker suspicion than the Jews, whom he had never much trusted under the best of circumstances. Each day the king found new ways of making their lives miserable, and this of course was what cast the deepest shadow of all on Tobit's happiness.

No longer was he welcomed to the balcony with his great-grandchildren to watch parades. No longer was it even safe to carry his baskets to the poor lest it be thought he was smuggling them weapons for an armed insurrection. Jews were spat at in the streets. Anna was insulted about her hair in the market. Worst of all, the executions began again even worse than before, and Tobit lay awake hours every night thinking about the strangled bodies thrown into the street with no one to bury them. He wondered what his people had done to bring the Holy One's wrath down upon them although even one of his great-grandsons could have told him that the whole thing had come about solely through the machinations of Nadab.

Fortunately for all concerned, the king came in time to find out that the letters were forgeries and let it be known that if Ahikar chose to come back out of hiding, his old job would be waiting for him. That was of course what Ahikar promptly did, and in no time at all the mistreatment of the Jews ceased as suddenly as it had begun, and once again Tobit slept the nights through like a baby. When he wondered what Ahikar had done to bring about this wonderful reversal of fortune, he decided that the Holy One must have been paying special attention whenever he distributed the king's semiannual bounty to the poor and had rewarded him accordingly.

Tobit lived to the age of one hundred and fifty-eight, or so it is believed, so when he started to feel in his bones that the end was approaching, it caused him neither surprise nor particular sadness. He couldn't think of anything he still wanted to see that he hadn't already seen or anything he wanted to do that he hadn't either already done or thought would be imprudent to do at his age or beyond his diminishing powers. He was ready to go when the time came, and if there was a life beyond this one as some people believed, maybe the Holy One would overlook all his many shortcomings and welcome him, and Anna too when her time came, into the second Jerusalem with its streets of beryl and ruby and the mysterious stone of Ophir.

In the meanwhile, he devoted his thoughts far less to himself and whatever lay before him than to the question of what was going to become of his people after he was gone and especially what was going to become of Tobias and his descendants. When he reached the point where he no longer even felt like getting out of bed in the morning, he decided to gather the whole crowd together for a last family meeting. Even the great-grandchildren were to be there, all of whose names and birthdays he continued to know as well as his own although for some months now he had tended to get muddled about which belonged to which. For the first time in weeks, he got himself fully dressed and joined them in the kitchen because it was the largest room in the house. Even so, most of them had to stand, some of them out in the courtyard with the door wide open so they could tell what was going on.

At least at the beginning, Tobias found that his thoughts were less on his father than on the dog. Returning to the house of his youth always made him miss him even though many years had passed by since he had seen him last. A brindled hare had gone racing across the grass one afternoon when he and Sarah were out on their terrace, and the dog had given chase. His intention was in no way to catch the hare because he knew if he managed it, he would have no idea what to do with him next. He simply thought it would be amusing to race around for a while with another creature who could more or less match his own astonishing speed. They circled the house several times and then ran up the hillside to the nearest outbuilding and back, and then, rather abruptly, the dog decided that he had had enough amusement to last him for a while and returned to the terrace with something less than the usual spring in his long legs and lay down on the flags. He was never to stand up again. It took Tobias a long while to get over it if he ever entirely did, and stepping back again into the kitchen for his father's meeting, he half expected to see that whiskered face looking up at him or to hear the thumping sound his long shanks made on the floor when he was nibbling for fleas.

The first thing Tobit said startled everybody because no one, not even Anna, had ever heard him say it before. His voice didn't carry as far as it once had, and many of them weren't sure they had heard him right, especially the ones in the courtyard.

"Tobias," he said, turning to his son who was sitting on one side of him with Anna on the other. "I want you to get out of Nineveh."

Tobias thought at first that the old man must be planning some new complicated errand he wanted him to run for him and wondered if conceivably Azarias might show up again to go with him, or whoever exactly it was that had been masquerading as Azarias because that was a point he had never been clear about, remembering only that he and Sarah had been frightened almost out of their wits by him when he had flamed up before them with such radiance that they had both been obliged to hide their faces in their hands. But Tobit soon made it plain that it wasn't a mere errand that he meant.

"I won't live to see it myself," he said, "but Nineveh is going to be wiped off the map. The prophet Jonah has said so, and besides that, I feel it in my bones. There won't be so much as a single stone left standing on top of another, and I want you to clear out before it happens and to take the whole family with you."

Tobias and his mother exchanged uneasy glances. Maybe Tobit was right, or maybe he was just going softheaded. In either case it gave them a sinking feeling in their stomachs.

"Where do you want me to go?" Tobias asked, and when Tobit didn't answer immediately, he repeated his question a little more loudly.

"I want you to go to Media," Tobit said. He had heard his son perfectly well the first time but had needed the pause in order to gather his thoughts together. "It won't be long before Media is wiped off the map too, but at least for a while you will be safe there. Your in-laws will be only too happy to take you in while you're hunting for houses of your own. Besides that, you also have come to have a fairly good head on your shoulders all in all, and you have plenty of money for making a fresh start."

Tobias thought it was no time to put up an argument, and Anna held her tongue too, because there was something in her husband's somber manner that gave her pause. His rather bleary eyes were staring into space as though he could see things beyond the range of the rest of them.

"There are stormy times coming," he said, and he narrowed his eyes a little as if the winds were already beginning to rise. "Our people will be scattered all over the world like dry leaves. Jerusalem will look as though an earthquake hit it. Solomon's temple will be left a shambles."

The meeting had to be suspended for a few minutes then because there was a disturbance in the back of the kitchen near the stove. One of the great-grandchildren had hit another with the same shoe that Tobit had used in the old days for swatting flies, and warfare had broken out with all the other children taking sides. It took the mothers some little while, but order was finally restored, and perhaps it was seeing everything return to normal that gave Tobit hope. In any case, he struck a more cheerful note when he started to speak again.

"The Holy One won't be angry at us forever," he said, "because that is not his nature. When he gets around to adding everything up, he will perhaps find that there aren't that many more points against us than there are points for us, and his mercy will make up the difference."

Remembering the long prayer he had once prayed when sitting on the rain barrel in the dark, he echoed some of the same language that he had used then for describing what form that mercy might take.

"The day will come," he said, "when he will bring us all back to our own true land and our comfortable homes. Jerusalem will be put together again, stone upon stone, and a new temple will be built that will make the old one look like an ant hill by comparison."

As in the prayer, he went on at some length about the

sapphires and emeralds that would sparkle in the walls, and the towers of pure gold and the rest of it, and all the while he kept waving his hand back and forth in time with the soft plucking of the harps.

"Even the godless will turn to the Holy One in the end," he said, and he let his voice drop so nearly to a whisper as he described this ultimate display of divine mercy that only those sitting closest could hear. "Even the Assyrians, what is left of them anyway, will smash their stone bulls to pieces. Even the Egyptians and Babylonians and the Medes will cast into the sea whatever disreputable images they happen to be carrying on with at the moment, and all peoples everywhere will join in singing the Holy One's praises to the end of time."

This more or less brought his speech to an end too, and his whole family, even the youngest, sat in silence for a few minutes as they wondered if what he had said with such conviction could possibly be true or was only evidence that his wits had turned. Tobias wondered especially if Nineveh was indeed going to be wiped off the map and if he and Sarah would have to pack up the whole crowd and somehow or other get them safe and sound to Media. There would be no Azarias to watch over them this time, he thought, and, worse still, there would be no dog trotting along at his side.

Sarah and the other women busied themselves then with passing around wine for the grown-ups and honey cakes and milk for the children while Anna helped Tobit climb back into bed because he felt that he had had enough confusion for one day and didn't care for anything to eat or drink anyhow. As he was drifting off to something like sleep, he marveled at how when he had prayed to the Holy One for death, the Holy One had given him instead not only life but the lives of all these other people who even now were tramping around his house and eating things.

When he died not very long afterwards at the age of one hundred and fifty-eight, if that figure is to be taken seriously, Tobias gave him a magnificent funeral, and when Anna died not long after that, he did the same thing for her. Needless to say, Ahikar graced both ceremonies with his distinguished presence, and at his suggestion the king sent some of his personal deaf mutes to enrich the general lamentation with the unearthly noises they made. On each occasion there was an elephant to draw the catafalque, and this was particularly pleasing to the children.

What remains to be told can be told quickly although it didn't happen quickly. After the death of his parents, Tobias decided that maybe he had better take his father's warning seriously and get out of Nineveh while the going was good. Sarah on her part was only too glad to leave because even after many years she still didn't feel entirely at home there and because she rejoiced at the thought of being reunited with Raguel, whom she had never stopped missing any more than he had ever stopped missing her. It was true that they had no Azarias to make sure they took the right roads or to get them through unforeseen disasters like the fish, but even though

they were aware of nothing more than an occasional unex-
plained flicker of light in the air as they went, they were of
course never altogether on their own.

Raguel's joy at their arrival can be easily imagined, and
even the larger of the two maidservants, who looked rather a
good deal less like a man than she had in her robust youth,
watched them draw up at the door with something that may
have been a welcoming smile on her face. As for Edna, she
practically stopped strangers on the street to tell them that her
married daughter had returned with more children and
grandchildren than she could count and a husband whose
wealth rivaled even that of Gabael, whom they all of them
remembered. This was entirely true, of course, because Tobit
had left his son all of the remaining silver, which was a very
large amount indeed, and it became truer still when Raguel
and Edna died and left him everything of theirs as they had
promised. Tobias threw both of them funerals that were fully
as spectacular as the ones he had thrown for his own parents
except that with no elephants to be had in Ecbatana he found
it necessary, much to the children's shrill dismay, to substitute
a number of richly caparisoned camels instead.

Just as Tobit had foreseen, Nineveh fell in due course
before the combined might of the Babylonians and the Medes,
and the body of the king was hurled off the very same balcony
where Tobit used to take his great-grandchildren to watch the
parades. Nothing remained of the mighty city except for a vast
collection of clay tablets on which all but the final chapter of

Assyria's hair-raising history was written for future historians to puzzle out as best they could.

Tobias had mixed emotions when he heard the news. On the one hand he knew how happy it would have made his father to see them get their comeuppance from the Holy One at last, and for his father's sake he tried to rejoice. But on the other hand he remembered all the good times he had had there over the years and all the interesting people he had met, such as the young woman who had given him the blue scarf. And of course he remembered most of all the dog, who had been a native Ninevite.

As he lay dying in his bed at what some say was the age of one hundred and twenty-seven, he was certain that he could feel him carefully taking his hand in his mouth in order to lead him to wherever it was he might be going next.